INTANGIBLE CULTURAL HERITAGE OF THE SOUTHERN SILK ROAD

神秘的南方丝绸之路 · 四川篇

——南方丝绸之路非物质文化遗产拾萃

主　编：陈思琦

副主编：李雨竹

参编：李佳　冷杉杉　王艳丽　刘怡然

西南交通大学出版社

·成　都·

图书在版编目（CIP）数据

神秘的南方丝绸之路：南方线绸之路非物质文化遗
产拾萃. 四川篇：汉英对照 / 陈思琦主编. —成都：
西南交通大学出版社，2020.10
ISBN 978-7-5643-7687-1

Ⅰ. ①神⋯　Ⅱ. ①陈⋯　Ⅲ. ①丝绸之路 – 非物质文化
遗产 – 介绍 – 四川 – 汉、英　Ⅳ. ①G127.71

中国版本图书馆 CIP 数据核字（2020）第 187934 号

INTANGIBLE CULTURAL HERITAGE OF THE SOUTHERN SILK ROAD

Shenmi de Nanfang Sichouzhilu · Sichuanpian
——Nanfang Sichouzhilu Feiwuzhi Wenhua Yichan Shicui

神秘的南方丝绸之路·四川篇
——南方丝绸之路非物质文化遗产拾萃

主编　陈思琦

责 任 编 辑	郭发仔
助 理 编 辑	吴启威
封 面 设 计	原创动力
出 版 发 行	西南交通大学出版社
	（四川省成都市金牛区二环路北一段 111 号
	西南交通大学创新大厦 21 楼）
发行部电话	028-87600564　028-87600533
邮 政 编 码	610031
网　　　址	http://www.xnjdcbs.com
印　　　刷	四川煤田地质制图印刷厂
成 品 尺 寸	170 mm×230 mm
印　　　张	9.5
字　　　数	181 千
版　　　次	2020 年 10 月第 1 版
印　　　次	2020 年 10 月第 1 次
书　　　号	ISBN 978-7-5643-7687-1
定　　　价	68.00 元

　　黑格尔说："亚细亚在特性上是地球的东部，是创始的地方。"这同样也是世界文明传播方向的隐喻。在人类的历史文化长卷中，有几条曲折蜿蜒的小路，跨过高山大海，直通欧洲，将东方美物的代表——中国的瓷器、丝绸和茶叶等商品输送到世界，这就是我们熟知的"丝绸之路"。

　　四川传说是嫘祖发明桑蚕丝绸的地方，也是中国丝绸最早的原产地之一。成都丝绸和"蜀布"在历史上享有盛誉，早在先秦时期，成都与印度、西亚各国、罗马帝国的商贾就有往来，主要就是将成都丝绸、蜀布等送去这些国家。而输送这些美物的逐步成型的通道在历史上被称作"南方丝绸之路"。南方丝绸之路以成都为原点，在秦汉时期初具雏形；在魏晋南北朝时期，由于北方战乱，其成为中国最为重要的对外贸易通道；到了唐朝高度繁荣，商贾不绝；而在明朝逐步衰落。在今天成都管辖范围内的邛崃市平乐古镇骑龙山脊和雅安市成佳镇，还残存着这条古道中的两段，它们见证着"南方丝绸之路"的辉煌历史。

　　俗话说："蜀道难，难于上青天。"无论是出川还是入蜀，南方丝绸之路都显得险峻又艰难。而探索和开拓这一条直通欧洲的商贾之道，需要多么巨大的勇气，多么执着的力

1

量，更是难以想象。这是蜀人的先辈们勇敢和力量的象征，更是这片"天府之国"上生活的人们心态开放、乐于交流的凝结，更展现了成都这一自古以来物产丰饶之地的重要商业文化传统和地位。

学界普遍认同的南方丝绸之路主要有三条，均以成都作为起点：一条为西线，经云南省通往缅甸、印度、中亚、西亚以至欧洲；一条为中线，经云南省至越南、中南半岛；另一条为东线，经贵州、广西、广东等省区至南海。

要讲南方丝绸之路，不得不提到"牦牛道"。"牦牛道"这个称呼是怎么来的呢？在汉代，大渡河之外的原住居民被称为"旄牛夷"，那里分布着邛、筰、冉龙等部落。蜀地的商人们带着天府之国的丝绸等物产，与大渡河外的旄牛夷、邛等部落交换牦牛、马等物，踏出了一条商贸之道，历史上便称之为"旄牛道"。历史上这条著名的路是从雅安名山（蒙顶山）出发，经雅州（雅安）、严道（荥经），翻大相岭，进入旄牛县（汉源）。到了汉源以后，"旄牛道"再分为两条线，一条经泥头驿（汉源宜东）去泸定，到打箭炉（康定），再往理塘、昌都、拉萨，以至西亚各国；另一条则经过邛都（今西昌）到云南，然后出国。而后一条路，也就是历史上的南方丝绸之路（西线）。

南方丝绸之路是中国历史上最早的对外贸易线路，也是中国与西方交流史上最早的陆路交通。经由南方丝绸之路进行的贸易，最早让西方了解中国，也最早让中国了解西方。在四川省广汉市发现的三星堆遗址和成都市的金沙遗址，距今已有5 000至3 000年的历史，是迄今在我国西南地区发现的范围最大、延续时间最长、文化内涵最丰富的古城、古国、古蜀文化遗址。而在其中发掘出的大量象牙、金器和玉器等文物明显是来自古代南方的南亚和东南亚的商品。这些出土文物足以说明，早在北方丝绸之路形成之前，一条连接中国和今天的孟加拉国、缅甸、印度、巴基斯坦、阿富汗和伊朗等国的商业通路，而这就是南方丝绸之路的开始。

南方丝绸之路在中国国内形成了西南及南方地区的巨大交通网络，在国外则与中南半岛、南亚、中亚、西亚连接成一个更大的世界性交通网络。南方丝绸之路涉及的广大地区是当今世界最具发展潜力的新兴市场，东南亚、南亚和西亚地区再加上中国，是覆盖人口超过 35 亿的巨大市场。2 000多年来，南方丝绸之路为连接中国西部与东南亚、南亚，特别是在促进双方经贸发展和人文交流等方面发挥了巨大作用。

南方丝绸之路作为一个学术命题提出于20世纪80年代，这一学术命题的提出实际上和当时社会需要关系极大，如李绍明先生介绍道："1987年中共中央第13号文件，号召重开'南、北丝绸之路'。四川省内学术界形成了成、渝为中心联系滇、黔两省共三支队伍，进行南方丝绸之路考察的活动。"

早在1987年之前，四川学术界便有学者对"南方丝绸之路"学术概念进行研究。在童恩正、李绍明两位先生的引导下，"南方丝绸之路"成为1985—1990年西南学术界研究的热点课题，并形成了一系列成果。早期"南方丝绸之路"的研究主要依托于西南地区考古学界和民族学界，这使得"南方丝绸之路"学术命题的研究具备多学科交流、合作，学术内涵丰富等特点。20世纪90年代中后期，三星堆遗址的重大考古发现，大大地丰富了"南方丝绸之路"的内涵，并开拓了"南方丝绸之路"研究的视野。这类研究充实了古代巴蜀文明借"南方丝绸之路"同外域文明的交流史实。进入21世纪，西南考古界不断地挖出重大遗址，其中以金沙遗址、十二桥遗址为重要代表，更加丰富了古蜀文明，同时也为研究古蜀对外交流情况提供了丰富材料，南方丝绸之路研究获得了充分的积淀，逐渐形成从国内走向国外，从区域走向整体研究的阶段。

南方丝绸之路（西线），从成都出发，途经邛崃、雅安、荥经、汉源、越西、喜德、西昌、德昌、攀枝花到达云南，从大理、宝山进入缅甸等东南亚各国。其中中国境内的四川、云南两省，是我国非物质文化遗产最为丰富的地区之一，两省共拥有国家级非遗243项，并有省级、州级、市县级非遗数千项。如成都市的蜀绣、漆艺；雅安市的荥经砂器、南路边茶制作技艺；凉山州的朵乐荷、彝族年；攀枝花市的苴却石雕刻技艺、仡佬族送年节等。丰富多彩的非物质文化遗产折射着这条几千年来形成的南方丝绸古道的文化变迁和历史兴衰，也使得这条古道散发着别具一格的特殊魅力。"神秘的南方丝绸之路——非遗中英普及系列读本"旨在将这些非物质文化遗产通过文字资料的形式，呈现到普通读者的面前，也通过中英双语的形式，将它们传播向更加广阔的范围。

由于南方丝绸之路上的非遗浩若星辰，数量十分巨大，故本册主要针对南方丝绸之路西线四川境内部分的非遗进行普及介绍。本册文字和插图均由"非遗中英互译读本——神秘的南方丝绸之路"社科普及课题组成员陈思琦、李雨竹、李佳、冷杉杉、王艳丽撰写、校对、绘制完成。我们以后将陆续推出其他分册，争取对此线的非遗进行全面的普及传播，将无尽的文化宝藏以图文并茂的生动形式呈现到大众面前。

在此，特别感谢四川省社会科学界联合会和四川非物质文化遗产教育传承与发展高水平研究团队对课题研究的大力支持！

陈思琦

2020年5月

Hegel said: "Asia is in the characteristics of the east of the earth, is the founding place." This is also a metaphor for the direction of the spread of world civilization.In the long history and culture of human beings, there are several winding paths which across high mountains and seas, straight to Europe, and transport the representatives of oriental beauty, such as Chinese porcelain, silk and tea, to the whole world. This is known as the Silk Road.

Sichuan is the birthplace of Lei Zu's invention of silkworm silk, and it is also one of the earliest origin of Chinese silk. Chengdu silk and "Shu cloth" enjoy a high reputation in history. As early as the pre-Qin period, there were commercial intercourse from Chengdu to India, West Asian countries and the Roman Empire. Among the transaction mainly merchant products were Chengdu silk, Shu cloth and so on to those countries. and the road which linking Chengdu and other countries ,sending these beautiful things above gradually become what we called the "Southern Silk Road." The Southern Silk Road took Chengdu as the origin and by inches began to become an archetype in the early Qin and Han Dynasties; in the Wei, Jin, Southern and Northern Dynasties, it became the most important foreign trade channel in China due to the war in the north; by the Tang Dynasty, it had reached its prosperity, and the merchants like an endless stream; and in the Ming Dynasty, it walked up to progressive decline . In the Pingle Ancient Town of Qionglai City and Chengjia Town of Ya'an City, which is under the jurisdiction of Chengdu today, there are still two sections of this ancient road, which witness the brilliant history of the "Southern Silk Road".

As the saying goes, "The road to Shu is harder than to climb the sky."Whether it is out or into Sichuan , the Southern Silk Road is steep and difficult, we cannot imagine how brave and persistent it takes to explore and develop this way of business leading directly to Europe. It is even more unthinkable. This is a symbol of the bravery and strength of the ancestors of the Shu people, and it is also the condensation of the people who live in this "land of abundance" with an open mind and a willingness to communicate. It also shows the important commercial culture tradition and status of Chengdu, which has been rich in products since ancient times.

It is recognized in academic circles that the Southern Silk Road consists of three routes, all of which start from Chengdu. The western route leads to Myanmar, India, Central Asia, West Asia and Europe via Yunnan; the middle route leads to Vietnam and the Indo-China Peninsula via Yunnan; and the eastern route leads to the South China Sea via Guizhou, Guangxi and Guangdong.

If we want to talk about the Southern Silk Road, we have to mention the "Yak Road." What is the origin of the "Yak Road"? In the Han Dynasty, the indigenous people living beyond the Dadu River in such tribes as Qiong, Ze and Ranpang were called "yak barbarians". The merchants of Sichuan traded their silk and other products for yaks, horses and other articles from the yak barbarians beyond the Dadu River; a trading channel called the "Yak Road" was thus formed. This famous road starts from a famous mountain in Ya'an (Mount Mengding) and enters Yak County (Hanyuan) via Yazhou (Ya'an), Yandao (Yingjing) and Daxiangling. The "Yak Road" forks at Hanyuan; one branch leads to Luding via Nitouyi (Yidong, Hanyuan), reaches Dajianlu (Kangding) and extends to Litang, Changdu, Lhasa and even West Asian countries; the other branch reaches Yunnan via Qiongdu (now Xichang) then extends abroad. The latter is the western route of the Southern Silk Road.

The Southern Silk Road is the earliest foreign trade route in Chinese history and the earliest land route in the history of exchange between China and the West, which enabling their earliest mutual understanding. The Sanxingdui Site in Guanghan of Sichuan and the Jinsha Site in Chengdu have histories of 3,000 to 5,000 years. They are ancient cities, ancient states and ancient Shu cultural relics with the largest areas, longest histories and richest cultural connotations discovered in Southwest China so far. A large number of artifacts found at these sites including ivory, gold and jade are obviously from ancient South Asia and Southeast Asia. These unearthed relics show that a commercial route, the Southern Silk Road, connecting China with today's Bangladesh, Myanmar, India, Pakistan, Afghanistan and Iran, formed long before the formation of the Northern Silk Road.

The Southern Silk Road formed a huge transportation network in the southwest and south of China, connecting with the Indo-China Peninsula, South Asia, Central Asia and West Asia to form a larger global transportation network. The vast area covered by the Southern Silk Road is the most promising emerging market in the world today. Southeast

Asia, South Asia, West Asia and China comprise a huge market with a population of more than 3.5 billion. For more than two thousand years, the Southern Silk Road has played an important role in connecting Western China with Southeast Asia and South Asia, especially in promoting economic and trade development and cultural exchange between the two sides.

The Southern Silk Road was proposed as an academic subject in the 1980s. In fact, the introduction of this academic subject was closely associated with the social needs at that time. For example, as Mr. Li Shaoming explains, "Document No. 13 of the CPC Central Committee called for reopening the 'Southern and Northern Silk Roads' in 1987. The academic circles of Sichuan Province organized three teams, namely Chengdu and Chongqing at the center, Yunnan and Guizhou, to investigate the Southern Silk Road."

As early as 1987, scholars in the Sichuan academic community studied the academic concept of the Southern Silk Road. Under the guidance of Mr. Tong Enzheng and Mr. Li Shaoming, the "Southern Silk Road" became a hot topic in the academic research of Southwest China in early 1985-1990s, and a series of results were obtained. Early research on the "Southern Silk Road" mainly relied on the archaeological and ethnological circles of Southwest China; as a result, research on the "Southern Silk Road" was characterized by multi-disciplinary communication and cooperation, and enriched academic connotations. In the mid-to-late 1990s, the major archaeological discovery of the Sanxingdui Site greatly enriched the connotations of the Southern Silk Road and broadened the vision of "Southern Silk Road" research. This type of research enriches the historical fact that the ancient Ba-Shu civilization communicated with foreign civilizations via the "Southern Silk Road". In the 21st Century, major archaeological sites have been discovered in the archaeological circles of Southwest China, including the representative Jinsha Site and Shi'erqiao Site, enriching ancient Sichuan civilization and providing abundant materials for the study of its external exchanges. With the accumulation of experience and knowledge, the study of the Southern Silk Road has gradually transformed from domestic to foreign research, and from regional to holistic research.

Starting from Chengdu, the Southern Silk Road (western route) reaches Yunnan via Qionglai, Ya'an, Yingjing, Hanyuan, Yuexi, Xide, Xichang, Dechang and Panzhihua, enters Myanmar via Dali, Baoshan and extends to Southeast Asian countries. Among them, Sichuan and Yunnan in China are among the areas with the richest intangible cultural heritage in China. The two provinces have a total of 243 national-level intangible cultural heritage items and thousands of intangible cultural heritage items at provincial, state, city and county levels, such as Sichuan embroidery and lacquer art in the Chengdu city; Yingjing grit utensils and the Southern Road Border Tea making process in Ya'an city; Duolehe and Yi New Year in Liangshan prefecture; and Juque Ink Stone engraving techniques and the Gelao New Year Gift Festival in the Panzhihua area. Such rich intangible cultural heritage reflects the cultural changes and vicissitudes of the Southern Silk Road over the past thousands of years, and endows this ancient road with a unique charm. The Mysterious Southern Silk Road – A Chinese-English Popular Book on Intangible Cultural Heritage aims to present this intangible cultural heritage to ordinary readers through textual collation and research in both Chinese and English, spreading it to a wider audience.

Due to the huge number of intangible cultural heritage items along the Southern Silk Road, this volume mainly introduces and popularizes selected intangible cultural heritage along the western route in Sichuan. The text and illustrations herein were prepared by members of the social science popularization group of the book, including Chen Siqi, Li Yuzhu, Li Jia, Leng Shanshan and Wang Yanli. In the future, more volumes will be published in order to fully popularize and spread the intangible cultural heritage of this route, and present the public with numerous cultural treasures in a vivid way.

Special thanks go to the Sichuan Federation of Social Science Associations and Sichuan Intangible Cultural Heritage Education, Inheritance and Development High-level Research Team for strongly supporting our research!

Chen Siqi

May,2020

目　录
contents

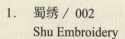

成都市 ──Chengdu City

成都市

CHENGDU CITY

鱼凫传说

夹关高跷

成都牛儿灯

成都漆器

1. 蜀绣

Shu Embroidery

第一批国家级非物质文化遗产名录

申报县区及单位：成都非物质文化遗产保护中心

Included in the First National Intangible Cultural Heritage list

Declaration county and unit: Chengdu Intangible Cultural Heritage Protection Center

《说文解字》释"蜀"字曰："蜀，葵中蚕也，从虫，上目象蜀头形，中象其身蜎蜎。"蜀国之所以得名为"蜀"，与蚕桑有很大的关系。传说蚕丛以蚕桑兴邦，领导古蜀人在成都平原栽桑养蚕，建立了国家，使这个原来以牧业为生的游牧民族的大部分人定居下来，跨入了农耕时代。尤其是经过开明治水和李冰创建都江堰，成都平原成为"天府之国"，农耕文化非常发达，为蚕桑丝绸的大发展奠定了良好的基础。

As we read in the *Shuowen Jiezi*, "The character '蜀'(shu) is like a silkworm in the sunflower; the '罒'(eye) in the upper part is like its head and the '虫' (worm) in the middle is like its body". The reason why the Shu State gained its name is closely related to sericulture. Legend has it that Cancong (Silkworm Twig) promoted sericulture, led ancient Shu people to plant mulberry and breed silkworms on the Chengdu Plain, and established the state, so most nomadic people who had previously lived on animal husbandry settled down and entered the agricultural era. Especially after Kaiming regulated the watercourses and Li Bing built Dujiangyan, the Chengdu Plain became a "land of abundance" with developed agriculture, laying a solid foundation for the grand development of sericulture and silk fabric.

　　蜀绣主要指以四川成都为中心的川西平原一带的刺绣。蜀绣早在晋代就被称为"蜀中之宝"，从而闻名于世。蜀绣以"色彩鲜艳、形象生动富有立体感"的图案闻名。1 000多年来，蜀绣逐步形成针法严谨、片线光亮、针脚平齐、色彩明快等特点。蜀绣的针法有十二大类，一百二十二种。常用的针法有晕针、铺针、滚针、截针、掺针、沙针、盖针等。蜀绣常用晕针来表现绣物的质感，体现绣物的光、色、形，把绣物绣得惟妙惟肖，如鲤鱼的灵动、熊猫的憨态、山川的壮丽、花鸟的多姿等。蜀绣的代表作为"芙蓉鲤鱼"和"大熊猫"。

　　"Shu Embroidery" mainly refers to the embroidery of the western Sichuan Plain with Chengdu at the center. As early as the Jin Dynasty, Shu embroidery was known as the "treasure of Shu"and famed the world over. Shu embroidery is well-known for its "colorful, vivid and three-dimensional"patterns. Over more than a thousand years, Shu embroidery gradually formed the characteristics of strict stitching techniques, bright pieces and lines, neat stitches and vivid colors. There are 12 main types of stitching technique in Shu embroidery which are divided into 122 subtypes. The most common stitching techniques include shading, placement, rolling, cutting, mixing, sand needle and covering. The shading technique is often used to accentuate the texture of the embroidery, vividly depicting its light, colors and images including agile carp, beautiful pandas, magnificent landscapes and flowers and birds in various poses. Representative works of Shu embroidery include "Lotus and Carp"and "Giant Panda".

2. 蜀锦织造技艺
Shu Brocade Weaving Techniques

第一批国家级非物质文化遗产名录

申报县区及单位：蜀锦织绣有限责任公司

Included in the First National Intangible Cultural Heritage List

Declaration county and unit: Shujinzhixiu company, ltd.

蜀锦，其起源于春秋战国，兴盛于汉唐，距今已有2 000多年历史。蜀锦专指以桑蚕丝为主要原料生产的具有地方风格（原古蜀郡，现成都市）的提花锦类丝织物。蜀锦常以多重彩经或彩纬起花，分为"经锦"和"纬锦"两大类。经锦工艺是蜀锦独有的。汉唐以前的蜀锦都是经锦，汉唐以后开始有纬锦。成都锦江赋予蜀锦染色得天独厚的条件，经草木媒染的绸或丝在江中洗濯，色泽更加鲜艳，色牢度更好。

Having originated during the Spring and Autumn and Warring States Periods, and flourished during the Han and Tang Dynasties, Shu brocade has a history of more than 2,000 years. It consists of a jacquard-like silk fabric with a local style (formerly Shu County, today's Chengdu city) produced with mulberry silk as the main raw material. The patterns of Shu brocade are made from multi-colored warp or weft silk, giving it two categories: "warp brocade" and "weft brocade". Warp brocade craft is unique to Shu brocade. There was only warp brocade before weft brocade emerged during the Han and Tang Dynasties. Jin River in Chengdu provides favorable conditions for brocade dyeing. After being washed in the river, the silk dyed with wood has brighter colors and better color fastness.

蜀锦纹样以花鸟卷草、瑞兽祥禽、云纹地域、人文景观为题材，受道教文化影响颇大。其图案构成有方形、条形、几何形纹及对称、连珠、团窠、四方连续等形式循环，装饰严谨、活泼新颖、奇异，形成多彩色丝显花的经锦与纬锦，也有经丝彩条起花、彩条添花，经纬都起花，既保持地方传统风格，又具有时代特色和生活气息。传统蜀锦以"赤、黄、青、白、黑"五方正色为主色调，红、绿、蓝、紫为间色，应用"晕裥炫色"的技艺，似"晕"似"云"，变化莫测，形成了蜀锦特有的风格。蜀锦织造技艺独特繁复，要完成一件蜀锦作品，需要经历纹样设计、定稿、点意匠、挑花结本、装机、织造等几个主要步骤。蜀锦的品种繁多，传统品种有雨丝锦、方方锦、铺地锦、散花锦、浣花锦、民族锦、彩晕锦等。

The patterns of Shu brocade mainly include flowers, birds, grass, auspicious beasts, clouds and human landscapes. Influenced by Taoist culture, the patterns are square, strip-shaped, geometric or symmetrical; there are also patterns in chains, clusters, quadrilateral continuums and other loops. The decoration is rigorous, lively and novel; patterns of warp brocade and weft brocade are presented in multi-colored silk; colorful warp silk and strips are also used for patterns; sometimes both warp and weft silks are used for pattern weaving, showing not only the local traditional style but also the characteristics and lifestyles of the times. Traditional brocade adopts "red, yellow, blue, white and black" as the main colors, and red, green, blue and purple as secondary colors. The technique of "shading and haloing"

is applied to make patterns which look like "halos" and "clouds", and are unpredictable, forming the unique style of Shu brocade. The weaving techniques of Shu brocade are unique and complicated. Several steps are required to complete a piece of brocade work, including pattern design, finalizing, layout arrangement, cross-stitching, loading and weaving. There are many varieties of silk brocade, of which traditional varieties include Yusi brocade, Fangfang brocade, Pudi brocade, Sanhua brocade, Huanhua brocade, Minzu brocade and Caiyun brocade.

3. 成都漆艺
Chengdu Lacquer Art

第一批国家级非物质文化遗产名录
申报县区及单位：成都市漆器工艺厂
Included in the First National Intangible Cultural Heritage List
Declaration county and unit: Chengdu Lacquer Art Factory

　　成都漆艺起源于距今3 000多年前的商周时期，是中国最早的漆艺之一。蜀地空气潮湿，气候温和，森林资源丰富，利于漆树的生长。自古以来，巴蜀就是漆的主要产地。除此以外，盛产的漆、麻、金、银、铜等天然美材和气候为漆艺的生产、发展创造了极为丰富的物质条件和有利的气候条件。早在汉代，蜀郡、广汉郡已是全国漆器生产中心，而中国长沙马王堆，朝鲜平壤王盱墓、古乐浪郡等地先后出土的汉代精美漆器，都刊有"成市草""成都饱""蜀都作牢""蜀都西工""成都郡工官"等铭文，它们都是当时成都漆艺鼎盛辉煌的佐证。

Having originated during the Shang and Zhou Periods more than 3,000 years ago, Chengdu lacquer art is one of the earliest lacquer arts in China. Sichuan is humid with a moderate climate and abundant forest resources, which are favorable conditions for the growth of lacquer trees. Since ancient times, Bashu has been the main lacquer-producing area. In addition, such rich natural materials as lacquer, hemp, gold, silver and copper, as well as the moderate climate, created extremely rich material conditions and favorable climatic conditions for the production and development of lacquer art. In the Han Dynasty, Shu County and Guanghan County were the national lacquerware production centers, and the Han lacquerware unearthed in Changsha Mawangdui Han Tombs, Wang Xu's Tomb in Pyongyang and Gulelang County are carved with such inscriptions as"Chengdu Grass" "Abundant Chengdu" "Made in Shu" "Shu Worker" and "Chengdu County Worker", which stand as evidence of the glory of Chengdu lacquer art at that time.

2006年，"成都漆艺"被国务院列入首批国家级非物质文化遗产名录，成都漆艺完整地保留了古老的传统技艺方式，以实木、大漆、矿物质原料、金银等贵金属为主要生产材料，形成制漆—制胎—底灰—髹漆—装饰—打磨—推光几大工艺，经几十至上百遍工序完成。

In 2006, "Chengdu lacquer art" was included by the State Council in the first National Intangible Cultural Heritage List. Chengdu lacquer art completely preserves ancient traditional techniques using solid wood, lacquer, raw minerals and gold, silver and other precious metals as its main production materials; the main processes include lacquer making, base making, bottom ash, lacquer coating, decoration, polishing and brightening. Dozens or even hundreds of processes are required to make a piece of lacquer work.

4. 成都糖画
Chengdu Sugar Painting

第二批国家级非物质文化遗产名录
申报县区及单位：成都市锦江区文化馆
Included in the Second National Intangible Cultural Heritage List
Declaration county and unit: Jinjiang Distrct Cultural Center, Chengdu

成都糖画，四川民间曾称其为倒糖饼儿、糖粑粑儿，它是用融化的糖汁作画的一种手工技艺，主要流传于四川省成都市及周边地区。糖画是一种既能品尝又能观赏的传统工艺品。据考证，糖画是在明代"糖丞相"制作技艺基础上演化而来的。据史书记载：在明代，每当新年祭祖时，官宦大户人家往往用模具印制糖狮、糖虎和文臣武将等形象用以祭祀。后来该技艺传入民间，逐渐演化为糖画。民间艺人在"糖丞相"基础上改进工艺，汲取传统皮影的制作特征及雕刻技法，不用印铸模具，而改为直接浇绘的方法。从此，一门独特的民间艺术"倒糖影"就诞生了。到了清代，糖画之风更加流行，制作技艺日趋精妙，题材也更加广泛，多为龙、凤、鱼、猴等普通大众喜闻乐见的吉祥图案。

Once known as "sugar cake", Chengdu sugar painting is a handcraft involving painting with melted sugar juice. Mainly localized to Chengdu and its surrounding areas, it is a traditional craft for taste and appreciation. According to the relevant research, sugar painting evolved from the production skills of the "Sugar Prime Minister" in the Ming Dynasty. According to the historical records, at the ancestor worship ceremony during the New Year in the Ming Dynasty, bureaucrats and wealthy families used molds to print images of sugar lions, sugar tigers and civil and military officials for sacrifice. Later, the craft was introduced to the common people and gradually evolved into sugar painting. The folk artists improved the craft on the basis of the "Sugar Prime Minister", took advantage of traditional shadow puppet production characteristics and carving techniques, and replaced printing by molds with direct casting. This gave rise to the unique folk art of "sugar cake pouring". Sugar painting grew in popularity during the Qing Dynasty when the craftsmanship became more and more sophisticated, and further themes were introduced; most of them were auspicious patterns that the general public liked, such as dragons, phoenixes, fish and monkeys.

2008年，成都糖画入选第二批国家级非物质文化遗产保护项目名录。糖画是一种蕴含了历史、美术、地方风俗、蔗糖工艺等元素的技艺。制作糖画时，要将制好后的糖置于铜瓢内加热融化，然后以铜勺为笔，以糖液作墨，在光洁的大理石板上，凭自己的技术和手法画出飞禽走兽、花鸟虫鱼、神话人物等形象。待新鲜的糖画凝固后，艺人用一根竹签把一件件作品黏合提拿起来，就完成了一幅作品，既可观赏又可食用。糖画制作有五大要素：一是要画得形象；二是线条要匀称；三是速度要快；四是要一气呵成；五是要掌握好等待取画的时间。糖画分为"大货""子货""丝丝货"和"小货"等。大货是指体型较大、构图复杂的作品，诸如龙凤、孔雀、狮虎、花篮、金鱼等。而小货是指体型偏小、工艺简单的作品，如单个的虫、鸟、水果等。子货即是直接倾倒的一个个圆形糖饼儿，这种技艺要求艺人手腕灵活，动作利索，倾倒过程中直接形成一个个状如纽扣的小圆饼，中间绝不拖泥带水，最能体现糖画艺人的基本功。丝丝货是以糖液所形成的缠绵的线条来构图，类似于国画中的白描和西洋画中的速写，又有中国民间剪纸的神奇韵味。

In 2008, Chengdu sugar painting was included in the second National Intangible Cultural Heritage List. Sugar painting is a craft which integrates such elements as history, art, local customs and sugar processing. To make sugar paintings, the prepared sugar should be placed in a copper scoop to be heated and melted; with a copper spoon as a pen and the sugar liquid as the ink, the artist then draws fowls, beasts, flowers, birds, insects, fish, mythical characters and other images on a smooth marble plate using techniques and skills. After the fresh sugar painting solidifies, the artist uses a thin bamboo stick to hold the pieces in one or two places, and completes a piece of work that can be enjoyed and eaten. There are five major elements in the production of a sugar painting: first, the image should be vivid; second, the lines should be smooth; third, it should be drawn quickly; fourth, it should be drawn in a single uninterrupted motion; and fifth, the drawing time should be controlled. Sugar paintings are divided into"large painting" "poured painting" "line painting"and"small painting". The large paintings are large and complex works such as dragons, phoenixes, peacocks, lions, tigers, flower baskets, goldfish and so on. Small paintings are small and simple works such as insects, birds, fruit and so on. Poured paintings are works made by pouring round sugar cakes. This technique requires the artist's wrist to be flexible and agile. During the pouring process, a small round button-shaped cake is formed directly, and no unnecessary steps are involved. Poured paintings fully reflect the artist's basic skills. Line paintings are composed of lingering lines formed by liquid sugar, similar to line drawings in Chinese painting and sketches in Western painting, with the magical charm of Chinese folk paper cutting.

5. 卓文君与司马相如的故事
The Story of Zhuo Wenjun and Sima Xiangru

第二批四川省省级非物质文化遗产名录
申报县区及单位：成都邛崃
Included in the Second Sichuan Provincial Intangible Cultural Heritage List
Declaration county and unit: Qionglai, Chengdu

　　卓文君与司马相如的故事，已有2 100多年的历史。是中国古代经典爱情故事。最早载于《史记》《汉书》，后成为历代诗词歌赋传颂的文学题材。

　　The story of Zhuo Wenjun and Sima Xiangru has a history of more than 2,100 years. It is a classic Chinese love story first recorded in *the Historical Records* and *History of Han Dynasty*; the story later became a literary theme in the poems and songs of many dynasties.

　　西汉时，蜀郡临邛有个才女，叫卓文君，貌美而聪慧，擅长诗画、音律。她的父亲卓王孙是当地首富。但卓文君受礼制约束，整天郁郁寡欢，常在月下抚琴，排遣心中的幽怨。司马相如，成都人，善辞赋，曾在京城入仕，游于梁，作《子虚赋》，名闻海内。司马相如回乡时，家贫无业，他的好友临邛县令王吉邀请他到临邛舍都亭。一天，卓王孙在家中设酒宴，邀请相如参加。席间，酒酣的时候，王吉请相如进琴，相如弹奏了一曲《凤求凰》表明对文君的爱慕之情。琴声婉转而深情，文君隔帘倾听，以心相许，便派仕女传信，互表爱慕之情。卓文君决定冲破礼教樊笼，去争取幸福和自由。一天夜里，卓文君与司马相如奔向成都，结成伴侣。卓王孙闻知女儿私奔，暴跳如雷，大骂女儿不守礼教，在经济上不给予夫妻二人任何支持。文君与相如在成都，家徒四壁，无以为生，便又返回临邛，变卖了车马，开了一家酒店。佳人才子肆中卖酒，立时轰动了全城。卓王孙非常生气，闭门不出，亲友一再相劝，要他看重相如才气，他才渐消怒气，分给文君一些奴仆和钱财。文君与相如离开临邛，重返成都，几年以后，相如再次进京入仕，写了《上林赋》《大人赋》等，成为著名文学家。之后，司马相如接受汉武帝委派，以"中郎将"身份，"建节往使西南"，经成都邛崃到今西昌、云南昆明一代，安抚边疆少数民族，为安定西南边疆、维护西汉统一做出巨大贡献。

During the Western Han Dynasty, there was a talented woman in Linqiong County named Zhuo Wenjun who was beautiful, intelligent and skilled at poetry and painting. Her father Zhuo Wangsun was the richest man in the area. However, bound by the ritual system, Zhuo Wenjun was depressed all day long. She often played the zither in the moonlight to dispel the resentment in her heart. Sima Xiangru, a native of Chengdu, was skilled in literature. He had once been an official in the capital and traveled to Liang. He was famed nationwide for his *Zi Xu Fu*. When he returned to his hometown, he was poor and unemployed. His friend Wang Ji, Head of Linqiong County, invited him to Shedu Pavilion in Linqiong. One day, Zhuo Wangsun gave a banquet at his home to which he invited Sima Xiangru. During the meal, Wang Ji asked Xiangru to play the zither. Xiangru played *Feng Qiu Huang* to show his love for Wenjun. This song is mild and affectionate. Wenjun listened secretly behind a curtain and fell in love. She sent her maid to deliver a letter to Xiangru declaring her love. Zhuo Wenjun decided to break free from the shackles of feudal ethics and fight for happiness and freedom. One night, Wenjun and Sima Xiangru went to Chengdu and got married without parental consent. Knowing that Wenjun had eloped, Zhuo Wangsun flew into a rage, cursed his daughter's violation of ethics and vowed to give the couple no support. Wenjun and Xiangru were utterly destitute in Chengdu, so they had to return to Linqiong. They sold their horse and carriage, and opened a wineshop. They sold wine in the wineshop which immediately stirred up the whole city. Zhuo Wangsun was very angry and stayed indoors. After his relatives and friends advised him to think about Xiangru's talents, Zhuo Wangsun gradually cooled down and sent Wenjun some servants and money. The couple left Linqiong and returned to Chengdu. A few years later, Xiangru went to the capital and became an official again. He wrote *Shang Lin fu*, *Da Ren fu* and other verses, and became a famous writer. He was also appointed by Emperor Wu of Han to "build relations with the southwest". He went to Xichang and Kunming via Qionglai to appease the ethnic minorities in the border areas, and made great contributions to the stability of the southwestern borderland and the unity of the Western Han Dynasty.

卓文君与司马相如敢于蔑视封建礼教，敢于冲破封建藩篱，赢得自由、美满、幸福的爱情故事也因此成为一段千古佳话。

The love story of Zhuo Wenjun and Sima Xiangru is a much-told story of despising feudal ethics, breaking through the feudal barriers and pursuing a free and happy life.

6. 鱼凫传说

The Legend of Yufu

第三批成都市市级非物质文化遗产名录

申报县区及单位：温江区文化馆

Included in the Third Chengdu Municipal Intangible Cultural Heritage List

Declaration county and unit: Wenjiang District Cultural Center

传说4 000多年前，一个崇拜鱼的部落和一个崇拜凫的部落结为部落联盟，迁徙到成都平原，经过征战建立了辉煌的古蜀鱼凫王国。这是个以农耕为主，以狩猎和渔业为辅的奴隶制国家。它拥有与中原地区相媲美的青铜工艺和堆积如山的财富。据史料记载和考古印证，温江可能是鱼凫王国的发祥地。鱼凫王及鱼凫王妃墓都在其境内，鱼凫村遗址更是被列为1996年全国十大考古发现。2001年，该遗址被列为国家级重点文物保护单位。鱼凫的传说故事很多，如"鱼凫架桥""鱼凫王大战饮马河"等。饮马河、鱼凫桥等河流、地名至今尚存。

Legend has it that more than 4,000 years ago, a tribe that worshipped fish and a tribe that worshipped wild ducks formed an alliance. After a period of war, they moved to the Chengdu Plain and established the glorious Yufu Kingdom. It was a slave state with farming as its main industry, and hunting and fishing as auxiliary industries. It had bronze craft and a mountain of wealth comparable to that of the Central Plains. According to the historical records and archaeological evidence, Wenjiang perhaps was the site of Yufu Kingdom, as the tomb of the Yufu King and his wife lies in its territory. In 1996, the site of Yufu Village was listed among the top ten archaeological finds in China. In 2001, the site was listed as a National Key

Cultural Relic Protection Unit. There are many legends about Yufu such as "Yufu Builds a Bridge" and "War at Yinma River". Rivers and place names including "Yinma River" and "Yufu Bridge" still exist today.

"大战饮马河"故事梗概如下：鱼凫王在温江建都以后，为了扩大疆域，又带领一些人到湔山去种他未下山前开垦过的土地。这时，川西坝上出现了另外一支人马，为首的叫獠伇子，勇猛剽悍。他趁鱼凫王不在国中，攻占了鱼凫城。鱼凫城北面有一条河，鱼凫王时常到河边放马饮水，大家都叫它饮马河。鱼凫王得到獠伇子攻占鱼凫城的消息后，立即率领人马赶回国来。刚到饮马河边，鱼凫王命令他手下兵卒，装成老百姓，晚上在河边烧香点蜡，大声呼喊："鱼凫王呀鱼凫王，你快点回来吧！獠伇子的人马都打过来了！"獠伇子听到呼声，以为鱼凫王没有回来，就带领人马连夜渡河，想再占领饮马河北岸土地。刚刚渡了一半人马，鱼凫王的队伍突然从河边冒了出来。鱼凫王一声令下，杀得獠伇子人仰马翻。獠伇子打了败仗，只得收拾残兵败将，朝南边逃跑了。鱼凫王这一仗大获全胜，非常高兴，回到鱼凫城后，立即下令奖赏：官兵酒宴三日，战马放饮三天。

The story of "War at Yinma River" goes as follows: after the Yufu King built his capital in Wenjiang, he led people to Jian Mountain to cultivate land he had previously exploited so as to expand his territory. At that time, another troop of people appeared in Western Sichuan, the leader of whom was Liaogezi, brave and fierce. Liaogezi invaded and occupied Yufu City when the Yufu King was away. There was a river in the north of Yufu City from which the Yufu King often let horses drink water, so everyone called it "Yinma River" (Drinking Horse River). Knowing that Liaogezi had occupied Yufu City, he immediately led his troops there. When they arrived at Yinma River, the Yufu King ordered his men to disguise themselves as civilians and burn incense and light candles by the river in the evening, crying loudly, "Yufu King, Yufu King, please come back! Liaogezi's troops are here!" Hearing these cries，Liaogezi thought that the Yufu King had not come back, so he led his men to cross the river at night, planning to occupy the land on the north bank. As the troops were crossing the river, the Yufu King's troops suddenly appeared at the riverside. When the Yufu King gave an order, his troops attacked. Suffering a crushing defeat, Liaogezi ran away to the south. Having swept his enemies away, the Yufu King was very happy. After returning to Yufu City, he immediately issued rewards: banquets were to be held for the officers and soldiers for three days, and the horses were to be allowed to drink from the river for three days.

7. 成都牛儿灯
Chengdu Cattle Lantern Dance

第三批四川省省级非物质文化遗产名录
申报县区及单位：大邑县文化馆
Included in the Third Sichuan Provincal Intangible Cultural Heritage list
Declaration county and unit: Dayi County Cultural Center

《新场乡志》（1810年编撰）记载：新场镇的潘茂山老艺人（已故）因被冤枉坐牢，在牢狱中学会了玩牛儿灯。第二年腊月下旬，潘茂山出狱返家，生活无以为继，约友人周平山创办牛儿灯。同年，牛儿灯就在大邑县其他乡镇兴起，之后周平山将牛儿灯传于子周泽云（已故）。由此，每年春节，周家牛儿灯就在新场镇和邻乡耍开了。

According to the *Annals of Xinchang Town* (compiled in 1810 the), Pan Maoshan (deceased), an old artist of Xinchang Town, was wrongfully imprisoned. During his imprisonment, he learned the cattle lantern dance. At the end of the twelfth lunar month the following year, Pan Maoshan was released from prison and returned home, where his life was unsustainable. He created the cattle lantern dance with his friend Zhou Pingshan. In the same year, the dance became popular in other villages and towns in Dayi County. After that, Zhou Pingshan passed the cattle lantern dance on to his son Zhou Zeyun (deceased). Since then, every year during Spring Festival, Zhou's cattle lantern dance has been popular in Xinchang Town and neighboring towns.

　　"牛儿灯"是农民秋冬农闲时节，以塑造耕牛形象为内容的一种娱乐活动。通过舞耍"牛灯"赞颂农民与牛的劳动生活乐趣。舞耍"牛灯"的人，一人扮使牛匠，戴斗笠、身披蓑衣、脚穿草鞋、背着牛草。一人扮赶牛么妹，牵牛、持牛鞭。两人扮耕牛，把制作好的牛头顶在头上，双手把道具篾撮口封好，身子前躬90度角，耍牛尾的人也前躬90度角，藏于道具下，扶住前人的腰。边舞边唱，唱腔唱词为地方山歌一类。

The "cattle lantern dance" is a recreational activity in autumn and winter for which the farmers create cow costumes. It praises the joy of labor and the life of cattle farming. One person portrays a cowboy wearing a hat, straw rain cape and sandals, and carrying cattle grass, while the other portrays a cowgirl leading a cow and holding a whip. Two persons play the cow; the one in the front wears a fashioned cow head, closes the costume with both hands and bends forward 90 degrees; the other person behind him bends forward 90 degrees, hides under the costume and holds the waist of the person in front. They dance and sing local folk songs.

　　牛儿灯以耕牛为载体，集造型、伴奏、伴唱、舞蹈为一体，载歌载舞，优美诙谐，地方特色浓郁，是川西民间舞蹈不可多得的原生态素材。是当地群众一种自娱自乐的形式，形式喜悦吉祥，提醒人们不忘农耕文化，对于弘扬优秀传统道德，建设和谐社会有着积极的意义。

With cattle as the carrier, the "cattle lantern dance" integrates craftsmanship, instrumental accompaniment, vocal accompaniment and dance. The witty and beautiful singing and dancing have rich local characteristics. Unique among folk dances in Western Sichuan, it is a form of self-entertainment for the local people which is joyful and auspicious, reminding people not to forget farming culture. It also has positive significance for carrying forward outstanding traditional ethics and building a harmonious society.

8. 人日游草堂

Visiting the Thatched Cottage on Human's Day

第三批四川省省级非物质文化遗产名录
申报县区及单位：成都杜甫草堂博物馆
Included in the Third Sichuan Provincial Intangible Cultural Heritage List
Declaration county and unit: Chengdu Du Fu Thatched Cottage Museum

"人日"又称"人胜节"，是全国性的节日，是我国的民俗活动之一。其历史悠久，在西汉时期已经形成，南北朝时期最盛，隋唐至宋已成春正大节，明清以来不断传承发展，辛亥革命后呈渐衰趋势。直到1992年，成都杜甫草堂博物馆为弘扬民族优秀的传统文化，首倡恢复"人日游草堂"的活动。"人日"（农历正月初七）这天，人们要吃七菜羹、游草堂、拜杜甫、吟杜诗、赏梅花、祈福新年。

Also known as "Human Victory Day", "Human's Day" is a national festival and Chinese folk activity. Formed in the Western Han Dynasty, it has a long history. It won great popularity in the Southern and Northern Dynasties, and was considered a great festival from the Sui and Tang Dynasties to the Song Dynasty. It was inherited and developed through the Ming and Qing Dynasties, and began to decline after the Revolution of 1911. In 1992, Du Fu Thatched Cottage Museum in Chengdu advocated resuming the "Visiting the Thatched Cottage on Human's Day" activity in order to carry forward the excellent traditional culture of the Chinese nation. On "Human's Day" (the seventh day of the first lunar month), people eat seven-vegetable soup, visit Du Fu Thatched Cottage, recite Du Fu's poems, enjoy plum blossoms and pray for the New Year.

　　"人日游草堂"则是成都独特民俗活动之一，其兴起于唐，迄今已有1 000多年的历史。最初主要是成都市各界文人雅士的文化生活内容之一，后此风气逐渐影响广大普通百姓。随着时间的推移，该活动的内容也不断丰富。现在，每年的"人日"期间（农历正月初一到初七），杜甫草堂都要举办丰富多彩的活动，在继承传统的基础上，还举办书画展、盆景展、梅花展，组织诗歌大赛、书法绘画比赛，开展灯谜游戏等，近年来还增加了登万佛楼敲钟祈福、成都故事·百家谈、草堂赛诗会、放河灯祈福、锦城唐风管弦乐演奏、唐代乐舞等内容。市民和游客不但可以在草堂感受到高品位的文化艺术氛围，同时也可以参与其中，亲身感受节日的喜悦。

　　"Visiting the Thatched Cottage on Human's Day" is a unique folk activity of Chengdu. It rose in popularity during the Tang Dynasty and now has a history of more than a thousand years. It was originally a part of the cultural life of scholars from all circles in Chengdu. Later, it gradually began to draw in the general public. As time went by, it was constantly enriched. Now, during each "Human's Day" period (the first to the seventh day of the first lunar month), a variety of activities are held at Du Fu Thatched Cottage. On the basis of inheriting traditional culture, it also hold calligraphy and painting exhibitions, bonsai exhibitions, plum blossom exhibitions, poetry contests, calligraphy and painting competitions, riddle games, etc. In recent years, more activities have been held, such as "Ascending Wanfo

Tower and Ringing the Bell for Blessings""The Story of Chengdu—Lecture Room""Poetry Contest at the Thatched Cottage""Floating River Lanterns""Jincheng Tang-style Orchestra", and "Tang Music and Dance". Citizens and tourists can not only experience a rich cultural and artistic atmosphere at the cottage, but also participate in the activities and experience the joy of the festival.

9. 四川清音

Sichuan Qingyin

第二批国家级非物质文化遗产名录
申报县区及单位：四川省成都艺术剧院
Included in the Second National Intangible Cultural Heritage List
Declaration county and unit: Chengdu Art Theatre, Sichuan Province

　　四川清音源于明末清初。康熙、雍正、乾隆年间（1662—1795），朝廷鼓励他地居民向四川大量移民，各地移民带来的乡音小曲，被四川唱曲艺人吸收，丰富了四川清音的唱腔和表演。四川清音在吸收各地唱曲并与本地方言相融合后，至道光年间（1821—1850），已发展得比较成熟。乾隆、嘉庆年间（1736—1820），随着商贸活动的日趋频繁，长江中下游一带的唱曲艺人，随商船溯江入川行艺，沿江商埠如万县、重庆、泸州等地唱曲卖艺甚为流行，这也促进了四川清音的发展。从四川清音曲牌中，可以看到它与省外许多地方的民歌小调的血缘关系。至此四川清音已基本定型的唱腔可分为"大调"和"小调"。"大调"即勾调、马头调、寄生调、荡调、背工调、越（月）调、反西皮调、摊簧调（艺人习惯称之为"八大调"）。唱腔结构有曲牌体（含联曲体、单曲体）和板腔体，共拥有两百余支曲牌。四川清音分布于四川汉族地区，曾称"唱小曲"。因演唱时多用月琴或琵琶伴奏，又叫"唱月琴""唱琵琶"。四川清音是唱的曲种，由一位演唱者一手执檀板、一手击节，站立演唱，琴师或小乐队伴奏，有时兼作帮腔。

Sichuan Qingyin is a musical style formed in the late Ming and early Qing Dynasties. During the reigns of emperors Kangxi, Yongzheng and Qianlong (1662—1795), the imperial court organized a large number of people to migrate to Sichuan. The local songs that these immigrants brought with them from all over the country were absorbed by the Sichuan singers and enriched the singing and performance of Sichuan Qingyin. The art form matured further during the reign of Daoguang（1821—1850） after absorbing songs and local dialects from various places. During the reigns of Qianlong and Jiaqing (1736—1820), as business activities became more frequent, singers from the middle and lower reaches of the Yangtze River went to Sichuan with the merchants, and street performances became particularly popular in such areas along the river as Wanxian, Chongqing and Luzhou, promoting the development of Sichuan Qingyin. From the names of Sichuan Qingyin tunes, we can see the relationship between qingyin and folk songs in many places outside the province. So far, two basic singing tunes have been formed for Sichuan Qingyin: the "major tune" and "minor tune". The major tune includes the "Gou Tune" "Matou Tune" "Jisheng Tune" "Dang Tune" "Beigong Tune""Yue Tune""Fanxipi Tune" and "Tanhuang Tune" (artists used to call these the "eight major tunes"). The structure of such operatic vocal music consists of the Qupai style (including joint style and single style) and Ban-qiang style, and there is a total of more than 200 tune names. Sichuan Qingyin is distributed throughout the Han area of Sichuan and was once known as "singing ballads". It was also called "singing yueqin" and "singing pipa" due to the accompaniment of the yueqin or pipa. Sichuan Qingyin is a kind of song performed by a singer who stands, holds hardwood clappers in one hand and beats time with the other hand, accompanied by a lyricist or small band, or sometimes a vocal accompanist.

　　从现存的四川清音曲目中，我们可以了解到巴蜀的风土民情、历史事件和风云人物。清音艺人常年奔走于城市乡镇或在茶楼设台演唱，或应邀去公馆出堂会，或到旅店为客人演唱。艺人们演唱的传统代表曲目有：《尼姑下山》《悲秋》《昭君出塞》《关王庙》《断桥》《思凡》《忆我郎》《绣荷包》《活捉三郎》《青冈叶》《小放风筝》等。四川清音还与四川扬琴和川剧相互影响，在吸纳融合了其他艺术精华后，最终成为具有浓厚地方色彩的曲艺品种。

　　From the existing Sichuan Qingyin repertoire, we can learn about the local customs, historical events and famous figures of Bashu. Qingyin artists travel around cities, villages and towns singing in teahouses, or they are invited to perform at private parties or sing for guests in hotels. The traditional representative songs of these artists include *Nun Going Down the Mountain*, *Sorrowful Autumn*, *Zhaojun Going Abroad*, *Guanyu's Temple*, *Broken Bridge*, *Worldly Pleasures*, *Missing Him*, *Embroidering a Pouch*, *Catching Sanlang Alive*, *Green Leaves* and *Flying a Kite*. Sichuan Qingyin also interacts with Sichuan Dulcimer and Sichuan Opera. After absorbing and blending with other artistic essences, it eventually became a kind of folk art with strong local colors.

10. 四川扬琴

Sichuan Dulcimer

第二批国家级非物质文化遗产名录

申报县区及单位：四川省曲艺团、成都艺术剧院、四川省音乐舞蹈研究所

Included in the Second National Intangible Cultural Heritage List

Declaration county and unit: Chengdu Art Theatre,Sichuan Quyi Troupe,Sichuan

Institute of Music and Dance

四川扬琴又称四川琴书，因其主要伴奏乐器为扬琴而得名。它来自四川民间，具有鲜明地域历史文化特色，它是典型的蜀音雅韵代表性曲种之一。清代乾隆年间（1736—1795）已见有扬琴伴奏的说唱表演，到嘉庆年间（1796—1820）才由多人分行当演唱，用荷叶（一面苏镲）击节伴奏，以渔鼓和檀板击拍，称之为"清唱扬琴"或"扬琴清唱"，俗称"渔鼓扬琴"。道光年间（1821—1850），艺人谢海楼首先将渔鼓改为盆鼓，俗称"大鼓扬琴"。到光绪年间（1875—1908），艺人谢兆松又将扬琴的梯形桥改为锥堞形，使上弦方便。

Also known as "Sichuan Qinshu", Sichuan Dulcimer is named after its main accompaniment instrument. It is derived from the folk circle of Sichuan and has distinctive regional historical and cultural characteristics. With its elegant rhymes, it is one of the typical representative forms of Shu music. During the reign of Qianlong in the Qing Dynasty (1736—1795), there was a talking and singing performance accompanied by a dulcimer. In the reign of Jiaqing (1796—1820), several performers sang and played different roles accompanied by the rhythm of lotus leaves (small cymbals), a yu drum and hardwood clappers; this was called "Cappella Dulcimer"

or "Dulcimer Cappella", commonly known as "Yu Drum Dulcimer". During the reign of Daoguang (1821—1850), the artist Xie Hailou first changed the yu drum to a basin drum to form a style commonly known as "Drum Dulcimer." In the reign of Guangxu (1875—1908), the artist Xie Zhaosong changed the trapezoidal bridge of the dulcimer to a cone-shaped bridge to make tuning easier.

　　四川扬琴一般有五个演员（即行话"五方人"），分为生、旦、净、末、丑等行当演唱，每人兼操一种乐器伴奏。演出时一般以坐唱为主，也可站立表演。扬琴表演形式有说有唱。唱腔分省调和州调。省调指成都市的四川扬琴唱腔，分"大调"和"月（或越）调"。大调是板腔体，有一字、快一字、二流、三板等板式；月调是曲牌体，有月头、叠断桥等曲牌近二十支。州调指成都以外地区的四川扬琴唱腔，属板腔体，有清板、二流、三板等板式。传统曲目有《将军令》《华容道》《闹宫》《醉酒》《秋江》《船会》《渔父辞剑》《哭桃园》《碧莲夜深》《仕林祭塔》等。

Sichuan Dulcimer is generally performed by five performers (i.e. the "five parties"): Sheng, Dan, Jing, Mo and Chou. Each person plays a musical instrument. The performers are seated or standing. The form of the performance includes talking and singing. The singing tune is divided into the provincial tune and state tune. "Provincial tune" refers to the singing tune of Sichuan Dulcimer in Chengdu, which is divided into the "major tune" and "yue tune". As the Ban-qiang style, the major tune includes "Yi Zi" "Kuai Yi Zi" "Er Liu" and "San Ban"; as the Qupai style, the yue tune has nearly 20 tune names including "Yue Tou" and "Die Duan Qiao". "State tune" refers to Sichuan Dulcimer tunes from outside the Chengdu and belongs to the Ban-qiang style, including such tunes as "Qing Ban" "Er Liu" "San Ban" and other Ban-qiang style types. The traditional repertoire includes *General's Orders*, *Hua Rong Dao*, *Intruding in the Palace*, *Drunk*, *Autumn River*, *Ship Club*, *Fisherman Refuses a Sword*, *Crying in the Peach Garden*, *Lotus at Midnight* and *Shilin Visiting the Tower*.

11. 新繁棕编
Xinfan Palm Fiber Weaving

第三批国家级非物质文化遗产名录
申报县区及单位：成都市新都区
Included in the Third National Intangible Cultural Heritage List
Declaration county and unit :Xindu District, Chengdu

新繁棕编是中国民间传统手工艺品之一，起源于清代嘉庆末年，至今已有200多年的历史。据文献记载，清代嘉庆末年新繁妇女即有"析嫩棕叶为丝，编织凉鞋"的传统。棕编是新繁农村妇女们在农闲时节增加收入的一种副业。在经济不发达的时期，新繁许多农户都靠棕编维持生活。20世纪30年代，新繁地区甚至出现了女子不会编棕编，出嫁都十分困难的情形。

Xinfan palm fiber weaving is one of the traditional folk handicrafts of China. Having originated in the last years of the reign of Emperor Jiaqing in the Qing Dynasty, it has a history of more than 200 years. According to the relevant literature, women in Xinfan in the last years of the reign of Jiaqing had the tradition of "dividing brown leaves into fibers to weave sandals". Palm fiber weaving is the by-work of rural women in Xinfan to increase their income during the slack season. In periods of economic underdevelopment, many farmers in Xinfan maintain a living by relying on palm fiber weaving. In the 1930s, it was even difficult for women to get married if they did not know how to weave palm fibers.

新繁棕编选材优良、季节性强，原料主要采用都江堰市（原灌县）、彭州市（原彭县）、大邑县、邛崃市等山区的嫩棕叶。每年4月，是艺人们采集嫩棕叶的最佳时节。用排针将叶划割成细棕丝，搓成棕绳，经硫黄熏蒸、晾晒、浸泡等工序，制成洁白、柔软的材料备用，或将部分棕丝染色备用，可作棕编制品的特殊装饰。编织方法有胡椒眼、密编、人字编等三种。棕编的提包多用胡椒眼技法，即将等距排列的经线相交叉成为菱形，再用2根纬线穿于菱形四角。鞋、扇类产品采用密编法。帽、席等多用人字纹。用木、纸、泥模型编制的包等产品，其上织饰花鸟兽等图案。用白净的素色棕丝编制的器物像绸绢般华美。有的用彩色棕丝以挑花、提花、织花等技法织成彩色装饰图案。

Xinfan palm fiber weaving is a seasonal craft which adopts superior materials, mainly the tender palm leaves of Dujiangyan City (formerly Guan County), Pengzhou City (formerly Peng County), Dayi County, Qionglai City and other mountainous areas. April is the best time for the artisans to collect tender palm leaves. The leaves are cut into fine palm fibers with a pin and rubbed into palm ropes. After sulphur fumigation, drying, soaking and other processes, they are made into soft white materials for use in the special decoration of palm fiber products.

The main weaving methods include the "pepper eye technique" "dense weaving" and "herringbone weaving". The pepper eye technique is mainly used for palm fiber-woven bags; that is, equidistantly arranged warp threads are crossed to form a diamond shape, and two weft threads pass through the four corners of the diamond. Shoes and fan products require the dense weaving technique. Caps, mats, etc. adopt the herringbone pattern. Such products as bags made on wood, paper and mud models have flower, bird and beast patterns. Products made of plain white palm fiber are as beautiful as silk. Some products have colorful decorative patterns woven with cross-stitching, jacquard weaving, flower weaving and other techniques.

制作过程中的产品造型均使用模型，模型可用木制、泥塑。主要品种为拖鞋、凉帽、椅垫、提包、凉扇、围棋盒、玩具等生活用品，以及飞禽走兽、花鸟虫鱼、戏剧人物等工艺品两类。其特点是比一般草编工艺品坚实耐磨，质地柔韧，体积轻便，造型优美，色泽明快，制作精巧。

Vital for the production process, the model can be made of wood or clay. The main varieties include shoes, summer hats, chair cushions, handbags, cooling fans, chess boxes, toys and other articles of daily use, as well as such artistic figures as fowl, beasts, flowers, birds, insects, fish and legendary characters. Generally more wear-resistant than straw crafts, they are characterized by their flexible texture, light weight, beautiful shapes, bright colors and exquisite craftsmanship.

12. 夹关高跷
Jiaguan Stilts

第三批四川省省级非物质文化遗产名录
申报县区及单位：邛崃市群众艺术馆
Inluded in the Third Sichuan Provincial Intangible Cultural Heritage List
Declaration county and unit : Qionglai Mass Art Museum

高跷起源于春秋时代，汉魏六朝称之为"跷技"，宋代叫"踏桥"，清代称之为"高跷"（又叫高脚灯）。《邛崃县志》记载：夹关高跷表演在清康熙年间，由于佛教盛行，庙宇广兴，出现在高竿会、平台会、挂生灯（许愿）等民俗活动中，多以鬼神形象出现。以后逐渐演化。到了1920年，夹关兴办了"三月二十八"庙会，每年此时为会期。是时春耕已备的农民常常合家出动，成群结队赶会，在酬神会又出现了"高跷灯"，表演高跷翻筋斗、翻五台山、爬高竿，在高跷上唱戏，成为迎神赛会上不可缺少的内容。

Stilts originated during the Spring and Autumn Period, and the practice was called the "stilt technique" in the Han and Wei Periods and Six Dynasties, "stepping on the bridge" in the Song Dynasty and "stilts" (also "tall lamp") in the Qing Dynasty. According to the *Qionglai County Annals*, during the reign of Emperor Kangxi in the Qing Dynasty, due to the prevalence of Buddhism and temples, Jiaguan stilt performance appeared in such folk activities as the "tall pole meeting" "platform meeting" and "lamp hanging" ("wish making"), mainly in the images of ghosts and gods, and it gradually evolved from there. In 1920, Jiaguan organized the "March 28th" temple fair and fixed this day as the date of the annual fair. Farmers

who had prepared for the spring ploughing often attended the fair in groups. At the ceremony for thanking the gods, such activities as "stilt lamp", stilt somersault, climbing Mount Wutai and climbing high poles took place; singing on stilts is still an indispensable part of the god-receiving event.

据传说，高跷灯还可以降妖除魔、求天降雨、保一方大吉。现在的表演主要目的是丰富和活跃群众的文化生活，主要表演形式是以口哨吹"一二一"及秧歌节奏作为表演步伐。高跷因肢脚较高，表演难度大，在表演时身上还要穿着较重的戏剧服装，手里拿着较重的演出道具，还要随着锣鼓、口哨、秧歌步伐的节奏进行表演，动作要协调，步伐要一致，是一种较难的表演艺术。

According to legend, the stilt lamp can also be used to ward off evil, pray for rain and protect the land. Today's performances aim to enrich and invigorate the cultural life of the people. The performance is delivered with a "one two one" whistle and a yangko rhythm. Stilt performance is difficult due to the long poles. The performer needs to wear a heavy drama costume, hold heavy props and perform to the rhythm of the drums, whistles and yangko. The movements should be coordinated and the pace consistent. It is a challenging performance art.

在漫长的岁月里，夹关高跷形成了独特的地方风格。作为反映本土的民俗风情和乡土文化的民间舞蹈形式，1998年，夹关镇被命名为四川省特色文化之乡——高跷之乡。

Over many years, Jiaguan stilt performance has formed a unique local style to become a folk dance form reflecting local folk customs and culture. In 1998, Jiaguan Town was rated as a Characteristic Cultural Town of Sichuan Province by virtue of its fame as the "Town of Stilts".

13. 都江堰放水节
Dujiangyan Tomb-sweeping and Water-releasing Festival

第一批国家级非物质文化遗产名录
申报县区及单位：都江堰市文体局
Included in the First National Intangible Cultural Heritage List
Declaration county and unit :Dujiangyan Culture and Sports Bureau

延续2 000多年的清明放水节（古代又称"开水节"），源于4 000年前的江神信仰和2 000多年前对江水的祭祀。据1974年对在都江堰渠首出土的李冰石刻像的铭文考证，至少在汉建宁元年（168），都江堰市民间就改祭祀江神和江水为祭祀李冰的春秋祭祀活动，形成辐射整个四川盆地的岁时节令民俗——清明放水节。

The over 2,000-year-old Tomb-sweeping and Water-releasing Festival (also known as the Water-releasing Festival in ancient times) originated from belief in the "God of the Yangtze River" 4,000 years ago and sacrifices to the river over 2,000 years ago. On the basis of textual research into the inscriptions on stone carvings of Li Bing unearthed in the Dujiangyan canal head in 1974, at least in the first year of Jianning of the Han Dynasty (168 AD), the people of Dujiangyan City changed from sacrificing to the God of the Yangtze River and the river itself to the Spring and Autumn sacrificial activities for Li Bing, forming the seasonal folk ritual Tomb-sweeping and Water-releasing Festival which is celebrated throughout the entire Sichuan Basin.

清明放水节是世界文化遗产都江堰水利工程所在地都江堰市的传统民俗文化。历史上，每年的清明节在都江堰都要举行隆重的放水大典，以预祝当年农业丰收，这是川西平原源远流长的传统习俗。届时，地方官员要亲自主持放水仪式，举行盛大的庆典活动。放水节初始于"祀水"。那是因为都江堰修筑以前，沿江两岸水患无常，人们饱受水患之苦，为了祈求"水神"的保护，常常沿江"祀水"。都江堰修筑成功后，成都平原从此"水旱从人，不知饥馑"，后人为了纪念伟大的李冰父子，将以前的"祀水"改为了"祀李冰"。当地群众也自发地组织到二王庙祭祀李冰父子，举办二王庙庙会，又称清明会。

The Tomb-sweeping and Water-releasing Festival is a traditional folk culture event of Dujiangyan City, which is also the location of the Dujiangyan Water Conservancy Project, a world cultural heritage site. In the past, the solemn Water-releasing ceremony was held in Dujiangyan on Tomb-Sweeping Day every year to celebrate the agricultural harvest of the previous year, and this was a longstanding tradition in the Western Sichuan Plain. At that time, local officials would personally preside over the Water-releasing ceremony and host the grand celebration. The Water-releasing Festival began with "sacrifices to the river"; this was because the people suffered greatly from unpredictable flooding before the construction of Dujiangyan. In order to pray for the protection of the God of the Yangtze River, the local people often offered "sacrifices to the river" along the banks. After the construction of Dujiangyan, the Chengdu Plain encountered less flooding and the suffering of the people was alleviated. In memory of the great Li Bing and his son, the people changed from their previous "sacrifices to the river" to "sacrifices to Li Bing". They also spontaneously went to the Two Kings Temple to offer sacrifices to Li Bing and his son, and held the Two Kings Temple Fair, which is also known as the "Tomb-sweeping Fair".

每到冬天枯水季节，人们在渠首用特有的"杩槎截流法"筑成临时围堰，维修内江时，拦水入外江，维修外江时，拦水入内江。清明节内江灌溉区需水春灌，便在渠首举行隆重仪式，撤除拦河杩槎，放水入灌渠。这个仪式就叫"开水"。唐朝清明节在岷江岸边举行的"春秋设牛戏"，就是最早的"放水节"。978年，北宋朝廷正式将清明节这一天定为放水节。

In the dry period of winter, the people built a temporary cofferdam in the canal head using the unique "Wooden Tripod Dam Closure Method", by virtue of which the water would be dammed into the outer river during maintenance in the inner river, and vice versa. During the Tomb-sweeping Festival, the irrigation area of the inner river called for spring irrigation, so a grand ceremony was held in the canal head at which the wooden tripod dam would be removed and the water released into the irrigation channel, giving rise to the "water-releasing" ritual. The "Spring and Autumn Bullfighting Drama Opera" that was held on the banks of Minjiang River during the Tomb-sweeping Festival in the Tang Dynasty was the earliest "Water-releasing Festival". In 978 AD, the government of the Northern Song Dynasty officially set the Tomb-sweeping Festival on the same day as the Water-releasing Festival.

清明放水节再现了成都平原农耕文化漫长的历史发展过程和民俗文化，体现了中华民族崇尚先贤、崇德报恩的优秀品质，具有弘扬传统文化的现实意义。如今，都江堰终年均可放水。但清明节放水的旧制仍是川西人民值得纪念的节日。作为一种古老的民俗文化传统和富有巴蜀特色的旅游观光项目，放水节砍杩槎活动仍每年如期举行。

The Tomb-sweeping and Water-releasing Festival reproduces the long historical development process of folk culture and agricultural civilization in the Chengdu Plain, reflects the excellent qualities of the advocacy of wise men and the morality and gratitude of the Chinese nation, and plays a role of practical significance in the promotion of traditional culture. Nowadays, Dujiangyan is able to release water all year round, but the old water-releasing system held during the Tomb-sweeping Festival remains a memorable holiday for the people of Western Sichuan. As an ancient folk custom, cultural tradition and tourism and sightseeing event full of Bashu characteristics, the wooden tripod dam cutting activity of the Water-releasing Festival is still held every year.

国家非常重视非物质文化遗产的保护，2006年5月20日，该民俗经国务院批准，被列入第一批国家级非物质文化遗产名录。

China has always attached great importance to the inheritance and protection of its intangible cultural heritage. On May 20th, 2006, with the approval of the State Council, this folk custom was included in the first National Intangible Cultural Heritage List.

14. 夫妻肺片传统制作技艺
Traditional Cooking Techniques of "Husband and Wife Lung Slices"

第一批四川省省级非物质文化遗产名录
申报县区及单位：四川省成都市饮食公司
Included in the First Sichuan Provincial Intangible Cultural Heritage List
Declaration county and unit :Chengdu FOOD Company, Sichuan Province

在清代末年，成都市井中出现许多提篮出售肺片的小贩。起初，有的是端个瓦钵，卖凉拌肺片，或将瓦钵放在长板凳一端，在其周围插上几双筷子，吃一片给你用小铜钱记一次，为平民小吃，但极不卫生。这时的"肺片"确实有牛肺。后来，因牛肺颜色难看，口感很差，所以经营者就取消了牛肺，成为无肺的"肺片"。由于名声很大，人们叫得久了，就沿用其叫法，无非是约定俗成罢了。成都卖肺片的小贩，多为流动性出售，其价廉物美，拥有众多的消费者。食者众，售者多，而最有名者莫过于"夫妻肺片"了。

In the late Qing Dynasty, many peddlers carried baskets and sold livestock lung slices in the marketplaces of Chengdu. In the beginning, some sold cold-dressed lung slices from earthenware containers or just put the earthenware container on one end of a bench with chopsticks sticking out. You paid one copper coin for one slice, constituting a snack for the common people which gave no consideration to hygiene. The "lung slices" at that time were made from bovine lungs. Later, the vendors stopped selling bovine lungs due to their awful color and poor taste, and the "lung slices" no longer consisted of lungs. Due to its high-profile reputation, people often talked about the dish and the use of the term was continued out of convention. The vendors selling livestock lung slices in Chengdu adopted the form of liquidity sales and won many customers due to the low prices and fine quality of their food. There were many fans and sellers of lung slices, the most famous variety of which was "Husband and Wife Lung Slices".

住在成都少城地带的郭朝华、张田正夫妻二人走街串巷出售"肺片"。不管白天夜晚，也不管吹风下雨，夫妻二人紧紧相随。他俩买回来做肺片的原料，清洗得干干净净，精选材料，制作也很精细，使人看见就产生好感；再用上好的调料，准确调味，拌出的肺片确实好吃，很有风味，深受欢迎。久而久之，人们为区别于其他人出售的肺片，遂将其取名为"夫妻肺片"。后来，郭氏夫妻赚了钱，遂在成都半边桥街，现人民公园后门右侧一个单间铺面设店出售，店名正式命名为"夫妻肺片"。后几经变迁，迁至闹市区的提督西街，扩大了经营面积，增加了牛肉面等食品，食者不光是品尝肺片，还可以有面食充饥，夫妻肺片成为一家中型的小吃店。开业以来，夫妻肺片从开门至关门，每天顾客如云，出堂者经营排起长队，等候购买肺片和家人共享口福。

Guo Zhaohua and Zhang Tianzheng wandered the streets of the Shaocheng area of Chengdu selling "lung slices". Regardless of day or night, wind or rain, the couple followed each other closely. The raw materials for lung slices that they bought were carefully selected and washed. Their delicate preparations gave people a good impression. The fine sauce and accurate seasoning made the mixed lung slices delicious, flavorful and popular. As time passed, people began to call their dish "Husband and Wife Lung Slices" to differentiate it from those of others. Later, Guo and his wife earned enough money to establish a single-room shop named "Husband and Wife Lung Slices" on the right side of the exit of People's Park in Banbianqiao Street. After several changes, they moved to Tidu West Street in the downtown area to expand their business, and added beef noodles and other dishes. People could not only enjoy lung slices but also noodles, so "Husband and Wife Lung Slices" became a medium-sized snack shop. Since its opening, "Husband and Wife Lung Slices" has had a crowd of customers from opening to closing time who often form long queues, waiting to buy lung slices and share them with family members.

　　夫妻肺片的厨师遵循严格的制作流程，如牛杂根据肚、心、舌等各自特点掌握加热时间，达到火候一致；卤熟的原料采取复制，特别是加以精制的陈年卤水调味，成品始终保持颜色红亮、软和入味、麻辣鲜香、细嫩化渣的特点。夫妻肺片成为成都市有口皆碑的著名食品。现在，夫妻肺片不仅为一种小吃而行市，而且常用作高级筵席的冷碟，受到中外客人的欣赏和赞扬。而夫妻肺片店也扩大经营规模，增加品种，成为成都市一家名店。夫妻肺片是成都众多名小吃中的佼佼者。

　　"Husband and Wife Lung Slices" chefs have always followed the strict cooking instructions. For example, the heating duration of the beef offal should be controlled on the basis of the characteristics of tripe, heart, tongue, etc. so as to attain consistent heat control. The marinated raw materials adopt purified matured brine for flavor, and the finished product should be bright red in color, soft and chewy, spicy and delicious, and delicate and smooth. "Husband and Wife Lung Slices" has become a legendary famous food of Chengdu City. Nowadays, it is not only a snack in the market but also a cold dish often served at high-level banquets, winning appreciation and praise from distinguished guests at home and abroad. The "Husband and Wife Lung Slices" shop has also expanded its business scale, added more varieties and become famous in Chengdu City. "Husband and Wife Lung Slices" is outstanding among the many famous snacks of Chengdu.

15. 竹麻号子

Dendrocalamus Latiflorus Munro Working Song

第二批国家级非物质文化遗产名录

申报县区及单位：邛崃市群众艺术馆

Included in the Second National Intangible Cultural Heritage List

Declaration county and unit : Qionglai Mass Art Museum

早在宋朝时期，平乐便以造纸业享誉海内外。《邛州志》中犹有"成都草纸半平乐"一说，就是说当时成都一半的草纸都是产于平乐，这一切成绩都归属于平乐辛勤劳动的造纸工人。而"竹麻号子"就是造纸工人在劳动时喊的一种劳动号子，时时流行，代代相传，距今已有上千年历史。竹麻号子主要流传在川西一带，尤以平乐同乐村的芦沟、金华村的金鸡沟、金河村的杨湾、花楸村广为流传。

As early as the Song Dynasty, Pingle enjoyed fame at home and abroad for its papermaking industry. The *Qiongzhou Records* show that Pingle rough straw paper accounted for half of the paper in Chengdu, and this achievement was owed to the hardworking papermakers of Pingle. The "Dendrocalamus Latiflorus Munro Working Song" is a song sung by papermakers as they worked which has been passed down from generation to generation for more than 1,000 years. It is mainly popular in Western Sichuan, especially in Lugou of Tongle Village, Jinjigou of Jinhua Village, Yangwan of Jinhe Village and Huaqiu Village of Pingle Town.

手工造纸一般要有二十人，在劳作过程中他们需要相互配合才能完成整个程序，当工人们感到疲乏或劳累时，就会哼唱竹麻号子，一旦有人起唱，其他工人就会随号子音调跟着唱，这时整个造纸作坊就会响起响亮的竹麻号子。繁重的劳动中，钩子手手执长钉耙，将需要打的竹麻交给工人打，同时唱号子，一领众和，以此来鼓舞干劲、统一节奏、抒发感情、消除疲劳。速度由慢到快，接近收工时，情绪达到高潮，非常热烈。在平乐千年造纸历史中，竹麻号子的唱调基本没有变，但唱词已变，其内容是随社会政治经济状况和生产生活方式的变化而变化的。竹麻号子唱腔原始、质朴，所有曲调包括高腔、平腔、连环扣、银丝调、扯麻花等。它的唱词内容丰富，乐段长短不一，随意性和伸缩性较强，常用"嗦咿咗""喂""哟嗬"等衬词，其中以传统的"数十二月"式最为典型。

Manual papermaking generally required twenty workers to cooperate with each other to finish all the procedures. When the papermakers became exhausted, someone would hum the Dendrocalamus Latiflorus Munro Working Song, others would join in with the melody and the entire papermaking workshop would soon be filled with a loud rendition. During tough work, the hook holder held a long rake, handed the raw material to the papermaker for processing and led the singing of the working song in order to motivate the team, unify the rhythm, express their feelings and eliminate fatigue. The song frequently speeded up and slowed down, and the papermakers grew passionate and enthusiastic toward the completion of their work. Throughout a thousand years of papermaking history in Pingle, the tune of the Dendrocalamus Latiflorus Munro Working Song generally stayed the same while its lyrics and contents changed according to social, political and economic situations, as well as production methods and lifestyles. The Dendrocalamus Latiflorus Munro Working Song has an original and simple tune, and its melodies include such modes as "high tune" "flat tune" "interlocking" "silver tone" "intertwining" and so on. The lyrics are rich in content, the time signatures vary and it has strong randomness and flexibility with padding syllables composed of "suoyizuo""wei" "yo-ho", etc., of which the traditional "Counting 12 Months" style is most typical.

后来，随着社会经济的发展，手工造纸逐渐被机器造纸代替，到20世纪80年代，平乐手工造纸业也已停止，但是竹麻号子作为一种民间音乐形式却并没有消亡，而是流传至今。

Later, with the development of the social economy, manual papermaking was gradually replaced by mechanized papermaking. By the 1980s, the manual papermaking industry no longer existed in Pingle Town, but the Dendrocalamus Latiflorus Munro Working Song was still sung and remains popular today.

16. 西岭山歌
Xiling Folk Songs

第四批国家级非物质文化遗产名录
申报县区及单位：大邑县
Included in the Fourth National Intangible Cultural Heritage List
Declaration county and unit : Dayi County

山歌，是山魂之音，也是山民的心声。数百年来，西岭山民往往以唱山歌为乐事。他们在春种秋收中，在守玉米防兽害的高脚棚中，在撕玉米的深更半夜，在烧碱、挖药、伐木等辛苦历程中，用山歌提神，用山歌传达情感，抒发旷达、乐观、坚韧、顽强、诚信、幽默、机智的坦荡情怀。由于西岭历史上曾为汉、藏、羌等民族杂居之地，西岭山歌的旋律色彩、调式也包含了汉、藏、羌民歌的一些元素，色彩鲜明，音域较宽，调子高亢，唱法自由空间较大，旋律较为特殊，山味、野味和民族风味颇浓。

Folk songs are the musical soul of the mountains and the voice of people in the mountains. For hundreds of years, people in mountains of Xiling have enjoyed singing folk songs. They sing to refresh themselves, convey their feelings and express their frankness, generosity, optimism, tenacity, persistence, integrity, humor and cleverness during the spring plantation and autumn harvest, in the high-foot shed where the corn is protected from animals, while peeling corn in the middle of the night, during the hard process of obtaining caustic soda and while gathering medicine or lumbering. Because Xiling was historically a place where Han, Tibetan, Qiang and other ethnic groups lived together, Xiling folk songs also include Han, Tibetan and Qiang elements in terms of their melodies, vivid colors and modes, wide ranges, resounding tunes, relatively free singing style, special rhythms, strong mountain themes and rich ethnic spirit.

西岭山歌大致可分为劳动、爱情、劝化（包括讽喻）、喜庆、祭祀、酒歌等。其唱式有独唱、领唱、和唱、对唱等，尤以独唱居多。词意富于比兴，乐句结构完整，音乐形象集中，其诙谐逗趣，令人开心愉悦。劳动类有唱和春种、秋收、挖药、烧碱、伐木、狩猎、放牧等。爱情类咏唱恋爱、求婚、夫妻情、反抗封建婚姻等。劝化类有警世、劝人求真务实、坚韧勤劳、惩恶扬善等。酒歌类以横山酒歌为著。喜庆类多用于红白喜事、节日时日。祭祀类有丧葬、祭祖、扫墓（此类歌词较少）。

Xiling folk songs can be roughly divided into songs of work, love, persuasion (including allegory), celebration, sacrifice, drinking, etc. Their modes include solo, chorus-led, chorus, antiphonal, etc., of which the solo is most frequently performed. The lyrics are rich in metaphors with complete structural phrases and centralized musical images of pleasing wit. Work songs are sung during spring plantation, autumn harvest, gathering medicine, obtaining caustic soda, lumbering, hunting, herding and so on. Love songs deal with love affairs, proposal, relationships between couples, opposition to feudal marriage, etc. Persuasion songs deal with caution, truth and practice, tenacity and hard work, warding off evil, promoting kindness, etc. Drinking songs mostly consist of Hengshan drinking songs. Celebration songs are mostly sung during weddings, funerals, holidays and festivals. Sacrifice songs are sung during funerals, ancestor worship rituals and tomb-sweeping (these have fewer lyrics).

西岭山歌歌词诙谐逗趣、粗放、野性，颇具刺激性、张力和感染力，耐人寻味。其音调高亢、原始、古朴、空灵，实属原汁原味原生态。其旋律流畅，节奏平稳，曲调可随词段多少而反复演唱。唱山歌不受时间、空间局限，颇具群众性和广泛性，既可自娱自乐，又可参与演唱、庆典、活动。其曲调明快，节奏鲜明。山歌讲究真情实感，其反映山民勤劳、朴实、不畏艰辛、追求真善美。山歌的情真意切和高洁情愫，正好为今人寓教于唱、寓教于乐提供内容和形式。西岭山歌存在于群众生产、生活、劳动中，是文化大餐中的原汁原味的民歌。

Xiling folk songs have humorous, rough, wild, thrilling, tensile, inspirational and intriguing lyrics. Their tones are resounding, primitive, simple and unsophisticated, unpredictable, original and natural. With smooth melodies and steady rhythms, the tunes can be sung repeatedly with different lyrics. Not limited by time and space, folk songs are both universal and popular. People can sing them for fun or take part in singing during celebrations and activities. The tunes are lucid and lively while the rhythms are relaxing and bright. Folk songs focus on real sentiments and reflect mountain people's diligence, simplicity, bravery and pursuit of true goodness, virtue and morality. They express true feelings, sincerity, nobility, elegance and emotion, offering contemporary people educational contents in delightful forms. Xiling folk songs have been present in the production, life and work of the people and they continue to offer an original cultural feast.

17. 成都道教音乐
Chengdu Taoist Music

第二批国家级非物质文化遗产名录
申报县区及单位：成都市道教协会
Included in the Second National Intangible Cultural Heritage List
Declaration county and unit : Chengdu Taoist Association

　　四川成都道教音乐也称川西道教音乐，是指流传在四川成都辖区内道教名山、宫观和各区市县的城镇、乡村中民间火居道坛使用的音乐。该音乐历史悠久，其源头可追溯至1 800多年以前东汉时出现的五斗米道斋醮科仪音乐。早期的道教科仪音乐，深受巴蜀古代巫教祭祀礼乐的影响。经过历代道教乐人的传承，现已发展演变为融南北道教经韵之精华，汇名山道观古雅与民间道坛通俗之风，具有浓郁川西地方风格的传统道乐。

　　Also known as "Western Sichuan Taoist Music", Chengdu Taoist Music is a popular form of music played in sacred Taoist mountains and temples in Sichuan, and Huoju Taoist folk altars in the towns and villages of various districts and counties. It has a long history, having originated from the Taoist ritual music of "Five-dou-grain Taoism" which appeared during the Eastern Han Dynasty more than 1,800 years ago. Early Taoist ritual music was deeply influenced by the sacrificial ritual music of ancient Bashu witchcraft. Having been inherited by generations of Taoist musicians, it has developed into traditional Taoist music which integrates the essence of the scriptures of both northern and southern Taoism, and gathers the elegant classical practices of Taoist temples in sacred mountains and popular folk Taoist altars, absorbing the strong local style of Western Sichuan.

成都道教音乐内容丰富，曲目众多，常用于道教的早晚功课和斋醮科仪活动中。一些早晚坛功课经音乐，一般由咏唱式韵腔、讽经腔、念咒腔和颂诰腔构成其基本框架。斋醮科仪音乐则由乐师的唱诵和经师的伴奏组成，传承分为教团传承和师徒传承。成都各宫观使用的常用韵曲，乐谱为当请谱和工尺谱，全凭道士口授心传的感悟。

With its rich contents and various forms, Chengdu Taoist Music is often played at Taoist events related to Taoism lessons in the morning and evening, as well as during Taoist rites. Certain morning and evening music for the Altar Sutra has a basic framework of singing, chanting, casting and admonishing. Music for Taoist rites is composed of chanting by the musicians and accompaniment by classics teachers, and the inheritance is divided into "order inheritance" and "apprenticeship inheritance". The rhymes and songs commonly used in various Taoist temples in Chengdu adopt "Dangqing" and "Gongchi" notation forms which are based on the insights of oral presentation and comprehension by Taoist priests.

四川成都道教音乐仍然保持以往形成的静坛和行坛两大流派格局。其中，静坛派，又称静居派，即全真道派。其道徒称为静坛派道士、静居道士、出家道士和住观道士。他们平时头上挽髻，身穿道服，不结婚，不茹荤腥，住在相对幽静的道观，过着集体且又安闲的宗教生活。该派使用的音乐属于全真道音乐系统，唱诵的经韵以属于十方韵的"北韵"为主，演奏的曲牌以细乐为主，掌握的音乐多数为声乐曲，较少是器乐曲，音乐风格古朴、淡雅，宗教气氛浓厚，具有明显的道观色彩。

In the Chengdu Taoist Music, the two major established schools of "Jingtan" and "Xingtan" are still maintained. Jingtan School, also known as "Jingju School", is a Quanzhen Taoist Sect. Its Taoists are called "Jingtan School Priests" "Jingju Priests" "Chujia Priests" and "Zhuguan Priests". They knot their hair, wear robes, never marry, observe a vegetarian diet, live in the relatively peaceful Taoist temple and enjoy a serene communal religious life. The music they play belongs to the musical system of the Quanzhen Taoist Sect, the scriptures they sing highlight the "North Rhyme" of the Ten Rhymes and the tune names they perform are characteristic of orchestral songs. The music they master is mostly vocal music with some instrumental music. It is characterized by a simple and elegant style, intense religious atmosphere and significant features of Taoist temples.

1979年，几位著名的高功和经师，如江至霖、刘理钊等，承担起培养下一代道教科仪音乐人才的重任，道教音乐于是得到恢复并逐步发展。2003年，青城山仙乐团和青羊宫道乐团相继成立，乐团成员共45人，已整理有60余支曲牌。

In 1979, several famous Taoist mages and classics teachers including Jiang Zhilin and Liu Lizhao undertook the task of cultivating the next generation of Taoism ritual music talents, thereby ensuring that Taoist Music would be inherited and continue in its gradual development. In 2003, the Qingcheng Mountain Xianyue Orchestra and Qingyang Palace Taoist Music Orchestra were established with 45 members and more than 60 arranged tune names.

雅安市

YA' AN CITY

南路边茶制作工艺

荥经砂器烧制技艺

荥经民间竹号

1. 荥经砂器烧制技艺
Yingjing Black Pottery Firing Craft

第二批国家级非物质文化遗产名录

申报县区及单位：四川省荥经县

Included in the Second National Intangible Cultural Heritage List

Declaration county and unit : Yingjing County, Sichuan Province

荥经古称严道，以砂器闻名。荥经砂器历史悠久，1982年，考古学家根据当地发掘的秦汉文物考证，早在2 000多年前荥经就有砂器生产。

Yingjing, whose ancient name was "Yandao", is famous for its black pottery. Yingjing black pottery boasts a longstanding history. According to the excavation of cultural relics of the Qin and Han Dynasties in Yingjing in 1982, black pottery production existed as early as 2,000 years ago.

荥经砂器的制作基本沿用历史遗留下来的汉族传统手工作坊生产方式，原始古朴的手工生产具有产品精致、独特、不重复等特性，同时也具有文物性特点。

The production of Yingjing black pottery basically follows the form and methods of a traditional handcraft workshop, producing delicate, unique and unrepeatable wares destined to become cultural relics.

荥经砂器制作工艺至今依然沿袭春秋时期的工艺，这种相传几千年的原始工艺，使荥经砂器形成了红色、银灰色、黑色为主的单色砂器，且以砂锅、砂罐等生活器皿为主。

Makers of Yingjing black pottery today still follow the methods used during the Spring and Autumn Period. By virtue of ancient techniques passed down for thousands of years, Yingjing black pottery is usually monochromatic with such main colours as red, silver-gray, black and so on, and its forms primarily include such household items as casserole pots, black pottery tanks and so on.

荥经砂器的原材料很简单，主原料是当地特产白善泥，与煤渣混合烧制而成。制作方式分为采料、粉碎、搅拌、制胚、晾晒、烧制、上釉、出炉、入库几道程序，环环相扣，不得出任何差错，如此才能制出一件满意的砂器。

The ingredients of Yingjing black pottery are simple. The main raw material is Baishan mud, a local specialty, and the black pottery is finally made on a fire with a mixture of coal cinders. The production process is divided into the following procedures: material collection, grinding, stirring, blank-making, sun-curing, firing, glazing, removal from the furnace and storage, with each step closely connected to the others. Satisfactory black pottery can only be made if there are no mistakes.

2. 南路边茶制作技艺
Southern Road Border Tea Making Techniques

第二批国家级非物质文化遗产名录

申报县区及单位：四川省雅安市

Included in the Second National Intangible Cultural Heritage List

Declaration county and unit : Ya'an City, Sichuan Province

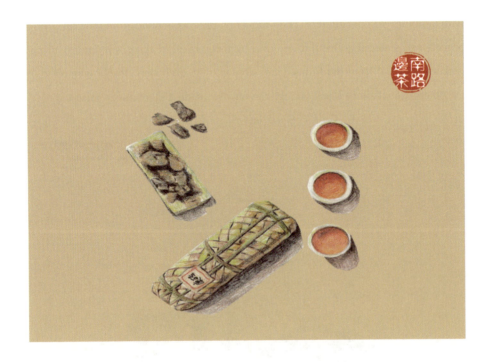

　　南路边茶，又称黑茶、乌茶、边销茶、南边茶、大茶、雅茶、藏茶，产于四川省雅安市，是黑茶的一类，距今已有1 300多年的历史，被誉为"西北少数民族生命之茶"。清朝中叶，"茶引制"改为"招商引岸制"，雅安及周边产茶县的口岸"批验所"设打箭炉（康定），因成都到该口岸须出南门，遂称此路所产茶为"南路茶"，南路茶绝大多数边销，故又称"南路边茶"。其从唐宋时就开始传承，形成一套独具特色的制作技艺和标准。南路边茶制作技艺主要分为采割、初制、成品茶加工三个部分。目前，一些工艺被完整保留下来，进行了改良完善。但很多手工操作的工具和用具正在消失、变异，能操作使用的人也越来越少。

Also known as "brick tea" "black tea" "border-selling tea" "southern tea" "big tea" "Ya tea" and "Tibetan tea", Southern Road Border Tea originated in Ya'an City of Sichuan Province. A kind of brick tea with a history of more than 1,300 years, it is honored as "The Tea of Life for the Minorities of Northwest China". In the middle of the Qing Dynasty, the "chayin policy" ("chayin" originally referred to the tea selling license) was changed into the "investment attraction port policy" (only allowing tea to be sold and bartered over at designated ports). Dajianlu (Kangding) was established in the Batch Inspection Office of the ports of Ya'an City and tea-producing counties. Because Chengdu City could only be reached via the southern entrance to the port, the tea produced along this road was called "Southern Road Tea", and most of it was sold along border areas, earning it the name "Southern Road Border Tea". This tea has been inherited since the Tang Dynasty, during which time a set of special techniques and standards were cultivated. The making process of Southern Road Border Tea is divided into three main parts: harvesting, initial production and finished tea processing. Currently, some techniques have been completely preserved and improved, but numerous hand tools have been disappearing and changing. Even worse, the number of people able to use them has been continuously dwindling.

3. 绿林派武术
Lulin Martial Arts School

第二批四川省省级非物质文化遗产名录

申报县区及单位：四川省雅安市雨城区文化馆

Included in the Second Sichuan Provincial Intangible Cultural Heritage List

Declaration county and unit : Yucheng District Cultural Center, Ya'an City, Sichuan Province

青城绿林派是清朝光绪年间起源于四川青城赵公山的一支传统武术流派，距今有120余年的历史。初以农民起义形式创派，融合中国传统武术南北二派之长，受中国侠文化思想影响甚大，又涵盖儒、释、道等传统文化思想特点，集技击、养生、修身、演练于一体。传统风格浓郁独特，尤以南派手法见长，在四川武术界享有"绿林小手"的盛名。

With a history of over 120 years, the Qingcheng Lulin School can be traced to a traditional martial arts school which originated on Zhaogong Mountain of Mount Qingcheng during the rule of Emperor Guangxu in the Qing Dynasty. This school was originally created for a peasant uprising, combining the advantages of the Southern and Northern Schools of traditional Chinese martial arts schools. It was also greatly influenced by traditional Chinese "Wuxia" culture and thoughts, including the traditional cultural philosophies of the Confucian school, Buddhism and Taoism. The art of attack and defense, longevity preservation, self-cultivation and maneuvers are integrated. With a unique and full-blooded traditional style, and especially being great at the tact of the Southern School, it enjoys the reputation of "Lulin Small Hand" in Sichuan's martial arts circle.

　　路军健作为传承人，使青城绿林派在雅安扎下了根，成为雅安流传最广、习练人数最多的一个流派。绿林派武术的形成受到了赵公山山高林密地带的环境与中国侠义文化思想及反清思想的影响，动作上体现出小巧多变，身桩、步法的变化，手上劲力的变化，路线的变化尽在其中。在打斗中也表现出侠家的快、狠，善于击打人体周身要害处，套路中也有很多包含反清思想的动作。绿林派武术以太极阴阳变幻为攻守。讲究式法自然，无神而不动，又莫贵于静也，静则心不忘动，而处之玉如，变幻莫测，神话无穷。

　　As the inheritor, Lu Junjian based the Qingcheng Lulin School in Ya'an City where it became the martial arts tradition with the largest number of practitioners and most extensive range. The formation of Lulin Martial Arts School was influenced by the dense forests and highland environment of Zhaogong Mountain, as well as Chinese chivalry culture and anti-Qing ideology. The movements reflect small changes in the posture and footwork, hand strength and routes. In fighting, it also shows the quickness and ruthless of the chivalrous with an art focused on striking vital parts of the body. There are also many movements in the routines that contain anti-Qing ideas. Lulin Martial Arts School uses the yin and yang of Taichi to change the tactics. It stresses natural methods, without movement until one concentrate his attention; although stillness is of the most importance, the heart does not forget to move; it is as unpredictable, mythical and timeless as jade.

4. 汉源彩塑

Hanyuan Painted Clay Crafts

第二批四川省省级非物质文化遗产名录

申报县区及单位：雅安市汉源县文化体育局

Included in the Second Sichuan Provincial Intangible Cultural Heritage List

Declaration county and unit : Culture and Sports Bureau of Hanyuan County, Ya'an City

汉源彩塑艺术上继承了古代泥塑的优秀传统，并有所发展和创新。它的作品内容选材自古典文学艺术，将古典文学艺术平民化，发展了民间艺术，使其创作具有雅俗合一的艺术特征。彩塑是以泥土为原料，以手工捏制成形的一种雕塑工艺品，其颜色或素或彩，其对象以人物、动物为主。制作方法是在黏土里掺入少许棉花纤维，捣匀后，捏制成各种人物的泥坯，阴干，涂上底粉，再施彩绘。

The painted clay crafts of Hanyuan County artistically inherit the fine traditions of ancient clay sculptures while adding certain advances and innovations. It's subjects are derived from the classic literary arts. As folk art developed along with the popularization of classic literary arts, the creation of painted clay crafts boasts the artistic characteristics of both elegance and mundanity. The raw material of painted clay crafts is mud. Kneaded by hand, a sculpted art ware piece takes shape. The art ware is either plain or colorful, with figures and animals being its themes. One creative technique is to add a few cotton fibers into the clay, stir it evenly, knead it into molded pottery, let it dry, apply the base powder and finally decorate it with colored paints.

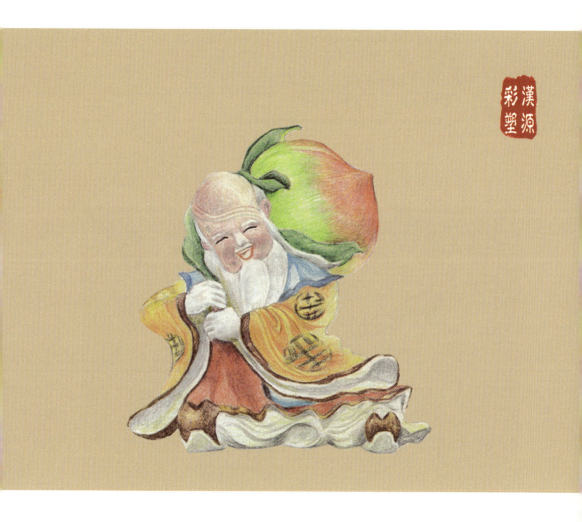

5. 荥经民间竹号
Yingjing Folk Bamboo Horn

第三批四川省省级非物质文化遗产名录

申报县区及单位：雅安市荥经县文化馆

Included in the Third Sichuan Intangible Cultural Heritage List

Declaration county and unit : Yingjing County Cultural Center, Ya'an City

旧时，荥经城乡周边，慈竹林随处可见。逢年过节、农闲休息，随手砍一根嫩慈竹便可制作一支竹号。吹奏竹号需要中气十足，这一要求也成为男青年展示自身力量和魅力的一种方式，于是竹号就成为人们，特别是男青年喜爱的一种自娱自乐的吹奏乐器。荥经竹号用料多为慈竹，20多节削好的大小竹筒，按从大到小的顺序连接而成，号体端直，长过一米，呈喇叭筒状，此状能将声音放得更大，传得更远。后竹号经过改良，由传统单音阶变成可吹奏乐曲的多音阶。

In the old days, ci bamboo groves could be seen everywhere in the countryside and urban areas of Yingjing, whether in fields or the corners of land. A tender bamboo shoot can be hacked to make a bamboo horn for the Spring Festival, festivals and slack seasons. Sufficient energy is required to play such a horn. For this reason, it has also become a way for young men to show their strength and charm. As such, the bamboo horn has become a kind of self-entertaining wind instrument that people love, especially male youths. Ci bamboo is usually adopted as the material for making a Yingjing bamboo horn. Over twenty sections of cut bamboo are closely linked according to their sizes. The body of the horn is straight with a length of more than one meter and a shape like megaphone, enabling the sound to be amplified and heard far away. Later, an improvement was made to bamboo horns that converted the traditional single scale into multiple scales, allowing more complex music to be played.

传统的竹号吹奏以刘文锦为首，在荥经人有喜事或是节气时表演。而改良后的竹号以廖建康为首，他带领大家吹奏出更响亮的竹号乐曲。

Traditional bamboo horn performances are led by Liu Wenjin, who plays whenever there is a wedding in Yingjing or a solar term approaches. Leader of the improved horns Liao Jiankang guides the crowd to play more sonorous music.

6. 抬阁（晏场高台）

Raising Sedan (Yanchang Town Hathpace)

第三批四川省省级非物质文化遗产名录

申报县区及单位：四川省雅安市雨城区文化馆

Included in the Third Sichuan Provincial Intangible Cultural Heritage List

Declaration county and unit: Yucheng District Cultural Center, Ya'an City, Sichuan Province

晏场高台是四川西部一种典型的可移动舞台艺术，距今已有400多年的历史，有着浓郁的本地民俗文化特色。晏场高台从400多年前单调、独一的地方戏走到今天复杂而多样化的高台艺术，通过巧妙的掩饰、复杂的找扎等技艺，根据故事的剧情要求，使历史文化人物通过高台活灵活现、栩栩如生地展示在人们面前。它是自发的一种民间文化，不仅有故事的趣味，而且有戏曲的风格；不仅有舞蹈的韵味，而且有杂技的绝招，有雕塑的形态和技艺的精巧；既有个人才艺展示，又注重整体动作的协调，充分表现了中华民族勤劳勇敢、团结向上的民族精神和万众一心，众志成城的凝聚力，体现了中华民族的文化具有深厚的群众基础和广泛的影响。

Yanchang town hathpace is a typical mobile stage art form in West Sichuan with a history of more than 400 years and rich local folk custom features. Over four centuries, this unique and monotonous local drama has developed into the current complex and diversified hathpace art. Through ingenious dissimulation, complicated papering and other techniques, historical and cultural figures and stories are presented to the audience in a lively and vivid way through hathpace. It is a spontaneous folk culture which not only has the taste of folk tales but also the style of opera; not only the charms of dance but also the tricks of acrobatics. It also involves the exquisite forms and skills of sculpture, as well as individual talent shows, and pays close attention to the overall coordination of movements. It is an art form which fully demonstrates the diligence, courage, unity, progress, cohesion and solidarity of the Chinese nation, reflecting the culture of the Chinese nation with a profound mass base and wide-ranging influence.

7. 花灯（芦山花灯）

Festival Lantern Play (Lushan Festival Lantern Play)

第二批四川省省级非物质文化遗产扩展项目名录

申报县区及单位：雅安市芦山县文化馆

Included in the Second Sichuan Provincial Intangible Cultural Heritage Extension Project List

Declaration county and unit : Lushan County Cultural Center, Ya'an City, Sichuan Province

芦山花灯属于四川地方灯戏，芦山县官方引用的专家意见认为其兴起于汉，盛行于宋，已经有2 000多年的历史。花灯表演中主要角色有两人，一是丑角（俗称"花鼻子"或"三花脸"），二是旦角（俗称"幺妹子"）。在表演中，其眉眼、身段、步法、念白、唱腔等仍具有祭祀、驱邪的影子。所以，芦山花灯是"傩中有灯，灯中有傩"，是研究傩戏的活化石。清朝乾隆年间的《芦山县志》记载，芦山花灯在北宋时期已是"沿门讴俚曲"，很是兴盛。

The Lushan Festival Lantern Play is a form of local lantern play in Sichuan Province. According to some reserchers whose opinion was quoted by Lushan County government, Having originated in the Han Dynasty and gained popularity in the Song Dynasty, this play has a history of more than 2,000 years. The two main characters are the harlequin [commonly known as "huabizi" (stained nose) or "sanhualian" (the make-up area is limited to the center of the face)] and the female role (commonly known as "yaomeizi", which originally referred to the youngest girl in a family and now usually means "young girls" in the Sichuan dialect). During the performance, the expressions, figures, gaits, soliloquies, arias, etc. still retain connotations of sacrifice and warding off evil spirits. Thus it can be said that "The lantern play is in Nuo Opera, and Nuo Opera is in the lantern play" ("Nuo" refers to a ceremony for warding off evil spirits), making it a living fossil for the study of Nuo Opera. According to the *Annals of Lushan County*, during the reign of Emperor Qianlong in the Qing Dynasty, at the height of its prosperity during the Northern Song Dynasty, the Lushan Festival Lantern Play inspired "door-to-door festival lanterns".

看芦山花灯表演，观众无不对"花鼻子"（丑角）的奇特扮相感到吃惊。他不但反穿皮袄，而且还斜挎半边膀子。反穿皮袄是羌族的习俗，斜挎半边膀子是藏族的穿着，而表演者的唱词和念白又是地道的汉语。一个地方戏曲有多种民族风情，说明芦山花灯是民族融合的产物。

When watching the lantern play, no audience members fails to be surprised by the strange appearance of "huabizi" (harlequin). He not only wears his fur-lined jacket inside-out but also pulls off one sleeve to expose his upper arm. Wearing the jacket inside-out is the custom of the Qiang minorities, while the latter behavior is that of Tibetans. The performers' lyrics and narration are in authentic Chinese. Local plays show a variety of ethnic customs, indicating that the Lushan Festival Lantern Play is a product of national integration.

8. 家禽菜肴传统烹制技艺（周记棒棒鸡制作技艺）

Traditional Cooking Techniques for Poultry Dishes

(Cooking Techniques for Zhou Family Bangbang Chicken)

第三批四川省省级非物质文化遗产名录

申报县区及单位：雅安市荥经县文化馆

Included in the Third Sichuan Provincial Intangible Cultural Heritage List

Declaration county and unit : Yingjing County Cultural Center, Ya'an City

棒棒鸡以连肉带骨、香嫩麻辣为标志，是有名的川派凉菜，历史至少可追溯至1895年，距今已125年，其发源地在川西青衣江流域。而荥经老字号周记棒棒鸡自清光绪年间创立，百年间已传承五代。2011年，棒棒鸡入选四川非物质文化遗产，成为保护技艺。

"Bangbang Chicken" is characterized by chunks of meat with bones and a delicious spicy taste. It is a famous cold dish of Sichuan cuisine, the history of which can be traced back to 1895. It has been 125 years since it was invented in the Qingyi River drainage basin in Western Sichuan. Old-fashioned Zhou Family Bangbang Chicken has been inherited for five generations over the past century. In 2011, it was selected as an intangible cultural heritage of Sichuan and became a protected skill.

棒棒鸡得名源于木棒。从前鸡价甚高，于是鸡肉只能宰成小块出售，根据鸡的重量确定各部位可宰成多少块。骨重的部位宰大些，骨轻的宰小些，鸡脯肉单独开片。为了使客人不挑肥拣瘦，鸡肉要尽量均匀，于是就准备好一尺长的木棒，将刀刃按在原料上，用木棒敲击刀背，不偏不倚、一刀一块，这便是"棒棒鸡"得名的由来。

The name "Bangbang Chicken" comes from a stick. Chicken was rather expensive in the past, so it could only be sold in small pieces. To what extent the pieces of different parts could be cut depended on the weight of the chicken; big pieces were cut from chickens with heavy bones and small pieces for those with light bones. The chicken breast was separated alone. In order that consumers do not select among the pieces, the sizes of the chicken pieces had to be as similar as possible. To this end, a one-foot stick was prepared and the knife edge pressed onto the ingredients; knocking on the back of the blade, exact pieces were cut one by one. This is the origin of the name "Bangbang Chicken".

棒棒鸡制作流程：炖煮—冷却—宰制—摆盘—淋佐料—加冷鸡汁—成型，棒击拆切规整，鸡片拌料淋油15分钟后口感最佳——入口香辣嫩滑，花椒之凉麻穿皮透骨，回口为糊香及芝麻香，此时鸡之鲜、肉之弹凸显无遗，满溢唇齿、余味悠长。

The process of cooking Bangbang Chicken is as follows: stewing, cooling, cutting and cooking, plate presentation, adding seasoning and adding cold chicken sauce, and finally the dish takes shape. Cut the chicken into equal pieces, then stir the seasoning and add oil. It tastes best after 15 minutes with a spicy and smooth taste and texture. The numbness and coldness of the pepper penetrate your skin into your bones. The aftertastes include the fragrance of sesame and the heat of spices. The freshness and elasticity of the meat at this time are unmistakable, full of lips and teeth with a long aftertaste.

9. 尔苏木雅藏族《母虎历法》
Tigress Calendar of Ersu and Muya Tibetan Nationality

第三批雅安市市级非物质文化遗产名录
申报县区及单位：石棉县文物管理所
Included in the Third Ya'an City Intangible Cultural Heritage List
Declaration county and unit: Shimian County Cultural Relics Administration

《母虎历法》是记载历法的书，目前，石棉县蟹螺藏族乡尔苏、木雅藏族聚居村寨还在广泛使用该历法。尔苏语称 "ga xi bu"，木雅语称 "gai zi qie"，意为"算日子书"，用"母虎"来定名是由于历书的扉页是虎转四季图，以及每年的第一月和每月的第一日属虎。材质为纸质（系藏族民间手工纸），书中的彩色图画用矿物颜料绘画，目前仅存5本。该历法是尔苏、木雅藏族遵循的一个行为规范，包含了天文、气象、时令季节，同时包含了尔苏、木雅人在日常生活中约定俗成遵守的一些禁忌，主要用于该区域尔苏木雅人祭祀、建房、乔迁新居、婚嫁、丧葬、动土、祈福、出行、迁徙、栽种等测算最佳日子和时间。《母虎历法》其功用与夏历、殷历、周历等古代

历法和现在广泛使用的黄历有相似之处，具有非常高的科学、艺术、历史价值，对于了解尔苏木雅藏族的生产方式、生活习俗、宗教信仰、天文历法等，以及研究古代少数民族历法具有重要价值。

The *Tigress Calendar* is a book recording the days of the year which is still widely used in Ersu Village of the Xieluo Tibetan nationality and the settlement villages of the Muya Tibetan nationality. It is called "ga xi bu" in the Ersu language and "gai zi qie" in that of the Muya, which means "a book that counts the days". It is named after a tigress because the title page contains pictures of a tigress in all four seasons, and the first month of every year and first day of every month belong to the horoscope of the tigress. It is made of paper (traditional Tibetan handmade paper). The colorful pictures in the book are drawn with mineral pigments, of which only 5 still exist. This calendar is also a code of conduct followed by the Ersu and Muya people, including astronomy, meteorology and the seasons. It also contains certain taboos that they conventionally observe in daily life, mainly regarding calculating the optimal day and time for a sacrifice, house building, housewarming, wedding, funeral, grounding break, prayer, journey, migration, planting, etc. The functions of this calendar are similar to those of the ancient calendars of the Xia, Yin and Zhou Dynasties, as well as the Huang Almanac which is widely used today.

It has very high scientific, artistic and historical value, and is of great significance for understanding the production, living customs, religious beliefs, astronomical calendars, etc. of the Ersu and Muya Tibetan minorities, as well as ancient minority calendars.

10. 木雅藏族"什结拉布"
Muya Tibetan "Shijie Labu"

第三批雅安市市级非物质文化遗产名录
申报县区及单位：石棉县文物管理所
Included in the Third Ya'an City Intangible Cultural Heritage List
Declaration county and unit: Shimian County Cultural Relics Administration

木雅藏族舞蹈"什结拉布"流行于石棉县木雅藏族聚居的村落，每年当地的晒佛节（藏历冬月十五）晚上必须跳"什结拉布"。"什结"木雅藏语意为"面具"，"拉布"意为"跳舞"，"什结拉布"意为"跳面具舞"。该舞蹈需要11名成年男子完成，两人敲鼓和打钹，两人扮演一对年迈的夫妇，7人扮演7位年轻的姐妹。扮演者用头帕蒙住脸部。舞蹈演绎一家人的日常生活，有打荞麦、手推磨、放牛羊、剪牛毛、纺线、织布等反映木雅人辛勤劳作的动作。"什结拉布"是木雅藏族先民遗留给后人的优秀文化遗产，是先民们在长期与恶劣的自然环境的抗争中产生的舞蹈，它包含了木雅藏族的宗教信仰、风俗、历史等诸多信息，其文化艺术价值可与西方的古希腊戏剧和目前西藏流行的藏戏相媲美，具有非常高的科学、艺术、历史价值。

The Muya Tibetan dance "Shijie Labu" is popular in the villages of Muya Tibetan minorities. They perform this dance during the Shai Fo Festival (November 15th of the Tibetan calendar) every year. "Shijie" means "mask" and "Labu" means "dance", so "Shijie Labu" means "mask dance". A total of 11 male adults are required for the dance, with two drumming and playing cymbals, two playing the roles of an aged couple and the rest playing the roles of young sisters. The dancers cover their faces with handkerchiefs. This dance portrays the daily life of a family, including buckwheat harvesting, milling, herding cows and sheep to graze, cutting ox hair, doubling threads, weaving and so on, which reflects the laborious work of the Muya people. "Shijie Labu" is an excellent cultural heritage left by Muya Tibetan ancestors for future generations. It is a dance that was created by ancestors in their long-term struggle against the harsh natural environment. It contains the Muya Tibetan nationality's religious beliefs, customs, history and a wealth of other information; its cultural and artistic value can be compared with that of the ancient Greek drama in the West and Tibetan drama which is currently popular in Tibet. It has very high scientific, artistic and historical value.

11. 上里镇天灯节
Sky Lantern Festival in Shangli Town

第一批雅安市市级非物质文化遗产名录
申报县区及单位：雅安市雨城区
Included in the First Ya'an City Intangible Cultural Heritage List
Declaration county and unit: Yucheng District, Ya'an City

　　天灯，又称孔明灯。上里镇群众自古就有放天灯的习惯，每当重阳、清明、元宵等时节，群众自发性地用五颜六色的纸扎成灯笼状"天灯"，请一些本地秀才在灯上写下祝福、吉祥的话语，然后就利用热气球原理，在夜间将灯放飞,以此表达他们对美好生活的向往，对亲朋好友的祝愿，以及对已逝亲人的思念等。集体放飞天灯时，场面十分壮观，初如神兵天降、夜同白昼，后似繁星满天、银河下凡。古镇商家、小贩也破例通宵营业，太子坝上

古戏台前挤满了看社戏的群众，老人们把桌椅搬到坝上来，三五成群地休闲纳凉、谈天说地。

Sky lanterns are also known as "balloon lanterns". The residents of Shangli Town have a tradition of launching sky lanterns. Whenever the Double Ninth Festival, Tomb-sweeping Festival or Lantern Festival approaches, the people will shape colorful paper into "sky lanterns" and invite local scholars to inscribe them with words indicating blessings and auspiciousness. Finally, using the principle of fire balloons, they launch the lanterns in the evening to express their hopes for beautiful lives, wishes for their friends and relatives, love for passed relatives, etc. It is a spectacular scene when they launch the lanterns collectively, like immortals descending from heaven. The lanterns brighten the night so much that it looks like daytime, and the sky is so studded with stars it appears the Milky Way has come down to earth. The merchants and hawkers of the ancient town also break the rules and remain open all night. The ancient stage of the Princes Dam is crowded with people watching village dramas. Old people move their tables and chairs to the dam to relax and chat in the shade in threes and fours.

12. 马马灯
Horse Lantern Show

第一批雅安市市级非物质文化遗产名录
申报县区及单位：雅安市名山区
Included in the First Ya'an City Intangible Cultural Heritage List
Declaration county and unit: Mingshan District, Ya'an City

马马灯是一种边唱边舞、唱舞结合的民间文艺（灯彩）表演形式。它主要流行于川西，尤其是雅安、蒲江、邛崃等地。歌舞者主要由马牌（2人）、幺妹儿（2人）为主。在四川锣鼓的伴奏下，马牌与幺妹结对起舞。领唱者唱一段后用"踮扒子""急箭敏"等步伐舞蹈，耍"穿檐柱"及跑阵式"双八挂""九连环"等拜主家。马马灯唱词格调为"双句式"（上下句）。主旋律简单明快（用鼓槌曲牌伴奏更有它的独特魅力）。马马灯表演时，伴有中式彩灯4个。上书"庆贺春节""年年有余""五谷丰登""人寿年丰"等，借以烘托表演气氛。马马灯主要在春节期间表演。

The Mingshan District Horse Lantern Show is a form of folk art (colored lantern) performance which combines singing and dancing. It is mainly popular in Western Sichuan, especially in Ya'an, Pujiang, Qionglai and elsewhere. The singers and dancers are mainly "Mapai" (2 persons) and "Yaomeier" (2 persons). Accompanied by Sichuan gongs and drums, the Mapai and Yaomeier dance together. After the precentor sings a section, he bows to the primary household before pacing and dancing in the styles of "zhuaibazi" and "jijianming", and performs "chuanyanzhu", running-style "double eight-trigram" and "jiulianhuan", etc. The pattern of the lyrics is "double-sentence" (upper and lower sentences). The main theme is simple and clear (and the accompanying drumming has unique charms). When the Mingshan District Horse Lantern Show is performed, 4 Chinese lanterns inscribed with the words "Celebrating the Spring Festival""Every year is enriching""Grain harvest""Longevity and abundant yields of crops", etc. are displayed so as to heighten the atmosphere. This show is mainly performed during the Spring Festival.

凉山州

LIANGSHAN PREFECTURE

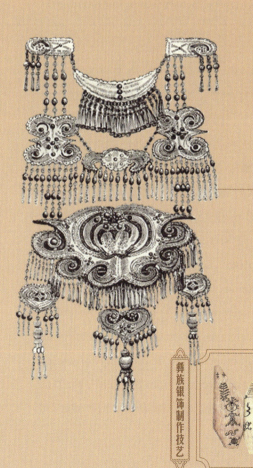

彝族月琴制作技艺

彝族漆器髹饰技艺

彝族银饰制作技艺

毕摩绘画

1. 彝族火把节

Torch Festival of the Yi Nationality

第一批四川省省级非物质文化遗产名录
申报县区及单位：四川省凉山彝族自治州
Included in the First Sichuan Provincial Intangible Cultural Heritage List
Declaration county and unit: Liangshan Yi Autonomous Prefecture, Sichuan Province

凉山彝族火把节，是彝族太阳历的第二个星回节，在每年农历六月二十四日举行。彝族火把节是四川十大名节，被联合国教科文组织列入"2010年世界非物质文化遗产审批项目"。四川省凉山州是我国彝族最大的聚居区。历史文献记载，火把节有"以火色占农""持火照田以祈年""携照田塍，云可避虫"等含意。火把节是彝族众多传统节日中规模最大、内容最丰富、场面最壮观、参与人数最多、民族特色最为浓郁的盛大节日。

Celebrated on the 24th day of the sixth month of the lunar calendar, the Torch Festival of the Yi ethnic group is the second Star Returning Festival of the year. Included by UNESCO in the "2010 Tentative List of World Intangible Cultural Heritages", it is one of Sichuan's top ten famous festivals. Liangshan Prefecture in Sichuan Province is home to the largest concentration of Yi nationality. According to historical documents, the Torch Festival involves "practicing divination on agricultural issues" "holding a torch and illuminating the field to pray for a good harvest" "holding a torch parade to drive away vermin from the field", etc. The festival is the largest, grandest, most colorful, most spectacular and best attended traditional festival of the Yi nationality.

　　火把节来历与彝族十月太阳历有关。该历法规定一个月为三十六日，一年为十个月，另加五日至六日为过年日，因此，它是太阳历，是以地球绕太阳为周期。彝族十月太阳历以十二属相之虎兔龙蛇马羊猴鸡狗猪鼠牛来轮回纪日。然而，随着农历的推广普及，现在的火把节不再依据太阳历，而是按农历来定时间。

　　The original Torch Festival was based on the Yi solar calendar. The calendar takes the 12 signs of the Zodiac as markers for counting days and includes 10 months with 36 days in a month, plus 5 to 6 days for the celebration of the New Year. As such, it is a solar calendar which takes the earth circling the sun as its cycle. However,with the popularization of the lunar calendar, the Torch Festival is now based not on solar calendar but on the lunar calendar.

　　每年的农历六月二十四日，凉山彝族同胞要穿上节日的盛装，载歌载舞，举办声势浩大的选美活动和服饰展示、赛马、摔跤、射箭等比赛，并在夜晚点燃火把在旷野中游行，纪念他们心中的英雄。

　　Every year on the 24th of June of the lunar calendar, the Yi nationality of Liangshan will wear festive costumes, perform songs and dances, and hold grand beauty pageants, traditional dress competitions, horse races, wrestling and archery matches, and evening torch parades to commemorate their heroes.

2. 彝族年

Yi New Year

第三批国家级非物质文化遗产名录

申报县区及单位：四川省凉山彝族自治州

Included in the Third National Intangible Cultural Heritage List

Declaration county and unit: Liangshan Yi Autonomous Prefecture, Sichuan Province

彝族年，彝语称为"库斯"，"库"即年、"斯"即新，意思是新年，是四川省凉山彝族自治州彝族传统的祭祀兼庆贺性节日。"库斯"一般选定在农历十月，庄稼收割完毕的季节。彝族年为3天。彝族年的头夜叫"觉罗基"，过年第一天叫"库斯"，第二天叫"朵博"，第三天叫"阿普机"。

The Yi New Year is called "Ku Si" in the Yi language, while "Ku" means "year" and "Si" refers to "new". For the Yi nationality of the Liangshan Yi Autonomous Prefecture of Sichuan Province, it's traditionally consists of days for offering sacrifices and holding celebrations. "Ku Si" is generally celebrated in October of the lunar calendar, the season of harvest. The Yi New Year lasts for 3 days. The Yi New Year's Eve is called "Jue Luo Ji", the first day of the New Year is called "Ku Si", the second day "Duo Bo" and the third day "A Pu Ji".

"年"的彝语为"库"，其意为：转、回、回转、回归、循环。彝族时空观念中一般把最北的端点作为起始点，太阳冬天日落点南移到最南端后，不再南移，在此停留几天后又往北移。此端点称之为"布古"，意为"太阳转回点"。然后到夏季时太阳落点又移到最北的端点，就不再北移而回归南移，此端点称之为"布久"，意为"太阳回归点"。此后日渐南移，到最南的端点。从最北的端点到最南的端点一个往返周期就是一年。

"Year" is "Ku" in the Yi language, which also means "to rotate, return or circulate". In the Yi space-time concept, starting from the northernmost point, the sun moves south to the southernmost sunset point in winter, where it stays for few days before again heading north. This point is known as "Bu Gu" or "the southernmost point to which the sun returns". Then, as the sunset point moves to the northernmost point in summer, the sun begins to head south again. This point is known as "Bu Jiu", or "the northernmost point to which the sun returns". From the northernmost point to the southernmost, the cycle takes one year, and the beginning of a new cycle falls around "Bu Jiu", the winter solstice of the Yi calendar.

3. 口弦音乐
Mouth Harp Music

第二批国家级非物质文化遗产名录

申报县区及单位：四川省布拖县

Included in the Second National Intangible Cultural Heritage List

Declaration county and unit: Butuo County, Sichuan Province

彝族口弦，彝语叫"红火"，是一种彝族特有的民间乐器。旧时，相互爱慕的彝族青年男女对弹口弦传情，以口弦相赠为定情信物。美姑县拉木阿觉乡美女峰下有一个口弦村——拉达村，据说，20年前，美女峰下的村民每家每户、男女老少都会"叮叮当当"打造口弦，并且每个人都会弹奏多首传统口弦乐曲。

Known as "Hong Huo" in the Yi language, the Yi mouth harp is a unique instrument of the Yi nationality. In the past, young Yi boys and girls affectionate to each other would send mouth harps to each other as tokens of their affection. The village of the mouth harp, Lada Village, lies under Meinü (beauty) Mountain in Lamuajue Town, Meigu County. It is said that twenty years ago, every villager despite age or gender could make mouth harps and play a great number of folk songs with the instrument.

美姑县民间口弦制作和弹奏传承人的阿哈介绍：凉山彝族口弦由最少一片到最多五片薄簧片组成，有竹片和铜片两种，簧片长5~8厘米，其中单片和两片的相对更长更宽一些，三片以上就会相对短小一些。弹奏时，竹制的和单片的音色更低沉、厚重一些，听起来宁静致远，时常会使人从心底荡漾起一股浓浓的乡愁感或忧伤感。铜制的和多片的音色相对清脆、圆润、秀丽，听起来使人欢快。

As explained by Aha, an inheritor of making and playing the mouth harp of Meigu County, the Yi mouth harp consists of 1 to 5 reeds of about 5-8 cm in length made from either bamboo or copper. The single-reed or dual-reed mouth harp is longer and wider, while a harp with more than 3 reeds is smaller. The bamboo and single-reed mouth harps produce deep and quiet music that often makes the audience sentimental or nostalgic, while the copper and multi-reed mouth harps make clear and mellow music that sounds joyful and lively to the ear.

4. 甲搓

Jiacuo Dance

第二批国家级非物质文化遗产名录
申报县区及单位：四川省盐源县
Included in the Second National Intangible Cultural Heritage List
Declaration county and unit: Yanyuan County, Sichuan Province

摩梭人主要分布在云南的宁蒗县及四川的盐源、延边和木里等几个县，人口约5万人。甲搓舞是四川凉山泸沽湖摩梭历史经典舞蹈，演员们以优美的舞姿展现出摩梭女人的勤劳、善良的品德，是国家第二批非物质文化遗产项目。摩梭"甲搓舞"俗称"锅庄舞"，是广泛流传于小凉山泸沽湖畔的一种民间舞蹈，具有较强的群众基础，每逢节日或婚丧嫁娶时，当地的少数民族都会自发地组织起来跳"锅庄舞"。甲搓舞的动作来源于摩梭人的劳动情形，共有72个动作。所谓甲搓，意思是为美好的时辰或时代而跳舞。作为一种群体娱乐性舞蹈，摩梭人会在庆祝丰收、节日、祈福神灵时跳起。害羞的摩梭男女如何在跳舞时相互表达心意？秘密藏在甲搓舞之中——他们通过跳舞时悄悄抠对方手心来倾诉爱意。甲搓舞是摩梭青年男女表白的"桥梁"，抠手心同样有讲究，只能抠三下，若对方同样有意，就会回抠。甲搓舞的基本步法有"前三步""后三步"以及"大跳"等，基本动作由腿部动作和手上动作构成，腿部主要表现为"跨退、踏步、辗转"等基本动作形式；手上动作主要表现为"摆、甩、晃、搭、撩"等。整个舞蹈动作先由慢到快，再由快到慢两大部分组成。众人手拉手按逆时针方向舞动。

The Mosuo people mainly live in Ninglang County of Yunnan Province, and Yanyuan, Yanbian and Muli counties of Sichuan Province, with a population of approximately 50,000. Also known as "Guozhuang dance", the Jiacuo dance is a typical historic custom and popular folk dance of the Mosuo people who live by Lugu Lake. The dancers portray diligent and kind Mosuo women with beautiful physical movements. It has been included in the second National Intangible Cultural Heritage List. As the people of local ethnic groups spontaneously organize "Guozhuang dance" performances for such events as festivals, weddings and funerals, this dance has a large number of followers. It's 72 dance movements have their origins in the labor practices of the Mosuo people. The word "Jiacuo" refers to dancing to celebrate good times. As an entertaining type of group dance, it is performed when the Mosuo people celebrate harvests and festivals, and pray for luck. How can shy boys and girls express their feelings? They secretly tickle the palms of their dream lovers when performing Jiacuo. As such, this dance is a bridge between young boys and girls. The rule is that one can only tickle another three times, and the other one will tickle back if it works out between them. The basic footwork of Jiacuo includes the "first three steps" "next three steps" and "jump". The basic movements are performed by the legs and arms. The leg movements include "striding backward, marking time, turning", etc., while the arm movements are "waving, swinging, swaying, placing, teasing" etc. The overall dance is composed of a slow-to-quick section and a quick-to-slow section. Everyone dances counterclockwise, holding hands with each other.

5. 彝族漆器髹饰技艺
Yi Lacquer Techniques

第二批国家级非物质文化遗产名录

申报县区及单位：四川省喜德县

Included in the Second National Intangible Cultural Heritage List

Declaration county and unit: Xide County, Sichuan Province

彝族漆器的特点是做工精制、造型多样、美观大方、笔法细腻、色泽对比强烈、通体绘纹、主次位置得当、繁简相宜、无异味、无毒、耐酸碱、耐高温、不变形、不易裂、不脱漆、精美大方。其华贵绚丽的纹饰和优美的造型浑然一体，和谐统一，其有浓郁的民族风情。

Yi lacquerware has such characteristics as exquisite workmanship, various shapes, elegant appearance, fine brushwork, strong color contrast, all-over patterns, proper position arrangement and balanced simplicity and complexity. It is also odorless, non-toxic, acid and alkali-resistant, high temperature-resistant, non-deformable, non-cleavable and non-depainting. Combining elegant and magnificent emblazonry with beautiful shapes, it has harmonious and exotic designs.

古代文献记载，彝族先民"随畜迁徙，毋常处"。为了游牧生活的便捷，彝族从一开始便选择了与生活相适应的轻便的木、皮、角、漆作为自己的日常生活用品之一。在凉山，木漆制品多选用不易裂缝、质地细腻、木纹较为统一的杜鹃树为料，以喜德、昭觉最为出名；皮漆、竹制品以美姑最为有名。其中水牛膝盖部分做成的彩饰皮碗最佳，是皮碗中的上品。

According to ancient documents, Yi ancestors "migrated with livestock but did not live in one place for too long". Living a nomadic life, the Yi nationality chose light wood, leather, horn and lacquerware as their daily necessities from the beginning. In Liangshan, most of the wood and lacquer products are made of rhododendron wood that is strong and durable, fine in texture and uniform in grain, of which Xide and Zhaojue are the best-known Producing places. As for lacquer and bamboo products, the most famous producing place is Meigu, where the best product among the best is the enamelled leather bowl made from buffalo knee.

漆器的色彩有红、黑、黄三色。彝族人民喜爱红色，它象征勇敢、热情；黑色代表尊贵、庄重；黄色代表美丽、光明。三色综合调配，间隔使用，色泽明快艳丽。漆器的纹饰特点是自然写实，纹样皆源于自然，来自生活。彝族漆器民族风格特别突出的造型，是鹰爪杯、雁爪杯、牛角杯和野猪蹄杯等饮酒器皿。这些酒器直接取材于自然物体，磨制彩绘而成，古朴自然，造型不凡。这些动物都凶猛、有力，为游牧狩猎民族所敬畏，借用它们的角、爪做酒杯，可以显示自己身份的高贵和势力的强盛。

The colors of lacquerware are red, black and yellow. The Yi love red, which symbolizes courage and enthusiasm, while black represents dignity and solemnity, and yellow represents beauty and brightness. These three colors are used simultaneously, creating bright and gorgeous effects. Yi lacquerware features natural and realistic decoration, with all it's patterns originating in nature and real life. The most distinctive shapes in Yi lacquerware can be found in such drinking vessels as the Eagle Claw Cup, Wild Goose Claw Cup, Horn Cup and Wild Boar Foot Cup. Polished, painted and inspired by the creatures of nature, they are primitive in an extraordinary way. Because these creatures are fierce, powerful and revered by nomadic hunter-gatherers, using their horns and claws to make wine glasses indicates dignity and power.

6. 彝族银饰制作技艺
Yi Silverware Making Techniques

第二批国家级非物质文化遗产名录

申报县区及单位：四川省布拖县

Included in the Second National Intangible Cultural Heritage List

Declaration county and unit: Butuo County, Sichuan Province

据考古发现，彝族是最早冶炼、铸造银器的民族之一。彝族人喜爱打扮，以佩戴金银为时尚，特别是崇银尚银的情结最为突出，这一习俗一直流传至今。这些传统的民风民俗不但使银器在广大彝族地区风靡，也造就了一大批手工艺者。

According to archaeological findings, the Yi are one of the earliest ethnic groups to smelt and cast silver. They love dressing up and wearing gold and silver. They particularly worship silver, and this custom has survived to modern times. These traditional folk crafts have not only popularized silverware among the Yi nationality but also created a large number of craftspeople.

凉山彝族银器种类繁多，有众多的银质餐具、酒具、马具、刀具、宗教用具和佩饰等，有的则在漆器上包上一层银皮或镶嵌银片，增加漆器的美观和价值。银器的纹饰手法采用阴刻、镂空、镶嵌等，较之漆器有了很大的进步。这些精致的银器所体现的美，是彝族手工业的精髓。

Yi silverware has a wide variety including silver tableware, wine accessories, horse accessories, knives, religious accessories, etc. Silver is also used to coat or inlay into lacquerware so as to increase its beauty and value. The silverware decoration techniques include intaglio, hollowing-out, inlay, etc., which are more advanced than those for lacquerware. The beauty that unfolds is the essence of Yi handicrafts.

在彝族群众中，男女老少均以佩戴银饰为贵，因此，人们用各种银饰装扮自己。可以毫不夸张地说，一个盛装的彝族女子，从头到脚，映入眼帘的都是琳琅满目、熠熠生辉的银饰。在彝族女子的穿戴中最贵重的是结婚用的"扯扯火"（胸饰）和"窝嘎"（背饰）。华美的胸饰已成为彝族银饰中的珍品。胸饰一般长达1米，一般需用纯银10多斤，由6至8件独立的饰件组合而成，用纯银链连接成环状。每个饰件垂吊筒穗、银铃。饰件上的图案丰富多彩，由太阳、月亮、星星、羊角、蝴蝶、麒麟、飞鸟、火轮等纹饰组成，整个图案形象突出、夸张，做工精细、纹饰外凸，颇富立体感。彝族男子一般喜在左耳佩戴大而粗的银耳环，有的男子也佩戴手镯和戒指，由此显示豪迈威武的英雄气概。

Silver jewellery is dear to the Yi nationality regardless of age or gender. They would wear silver upon silver. It is no exaggeration to say that a gorgeously dressed Yi girl can be draped in silver and glitter from head to heel. The most expensive accessories for women include the plastron "Che Che Huo" and back decoration "Wo Ga". Resplendent plastrons are the treasure of Yi silver jewellery. They can reach a length of 1 m. Generally they are made of more than 5 kg of sterling silver, and 6 to 8 pieces with tassels and tinkles are looped with sterling silver links. These decorative pieces are decorated with patterns of the sun, moon, stars, horns, butterflies, kylins, birds, burning wheels, etc. These images are outstanding, exquisitely made, and three-dimensional. Yi men generally wear a large thick silver pendant on the left ear. Some men wear bracelets and rings to show masculinity and heroism.

7. 婚俗（彝族传统婚俗）
Yi Marriage Customs

第三批国家级非物质文化遗产名录
申报县区及单位：四川省美姑县
Included in the Third National Intangible Cultural Heritage List
Declaration county and unit: Meigu County, Sichuan Province

订婚，彝语叫"吾让木"，是双方正式结缔婚姻的主要标志。订婚时，男方家择日携带白酒和春秋季同窝孵出的一对小鸡前往女家行聘。一般情况下，聘金可用现金或银子，但不能全给完，留下一小部分，以取细水长流之意。订婚后，双方不得轻易毁约。如果男方先毁约且已付聘金，则聘金不退；如果女方毁约，且已收聘金，在原聘金的基础上加倍赔偿。

Engagement, or "Wu Rang Mu" in the Yi language, is a milestone for a couple. To reach an engagement, the man's family goes to the woman's on an auspicious day and presents a betrothal gift, distilled spirit or a pair of chicks hatched in the same coop in Spring and Autumn respectively. A bride token can generally be offered in cash or silver, but not offered in full, symbolizing a frugal life after marriage. After engagement, the families cannot renege easily. If the man's family breaks the engagement, they will not have the bride token refunded; if the woman's family breaks the engagement, they should refund the token and also pay compensation.

美姑彝族至今还保留着婚前禁食的习俗。婚前一周，新娘每天只吃一个鸡蛋和喝一碗水，出嫁那天完全禁食禁水，彝语称叫"杂果"。过去，禁食时间越长，就越显得新娘懂礼节、有毅力。

The Yi nationality living in Meigu observe a pre-wedding fasting tradition. the bride should have only an egg and a bowl of water per day for the week before the wedding, and fast on the wedding day. This is called "Za Guo" by the Yi nationality. In the past, a longer time of fasting would indicate the bride's good etiquette and persistence.

美姑彝族结婚分"阿弥西"（嫁女儿）和"媳嫫西"（娶媳妇）两道仪式，"阿弥西"的承办方主要是女方家，"媳嫫西"的承办方主要是男方家。"阿弥西"也就是出嫁。女方家一般在出嫁前的一个星期左右，就开始举行"闹婚"。白天亲朋好友和左右邻居都聚集在女方家帮忙做活计，为出嫁的女儿准备结婚的嫁妆，绣项圈、绣花衣、穿玛瑙耳环、绣彩裙、做华服等，夜晚则是通宵的饮酒对歌、叙旧怀情。

In Meigu, a typical Yi wedding is made up two ceremonies: "A Mi Xi" ,or "sending the bride from her parents' family", and "Xi Mo Xi", or "greeting the bride at the bridegroom's family"; the former is hosted by the bride's family and the latter by the bridegroom's. In the week before a wedding, there is "horseplay" in the bride's home. During the day, relatives, friends and neighbors gather at the bride's home to help with the work, prepare the dowry, embroider collars, clothes and colorful skirts, and make agate earrings. During the night, the young people drink, sing songs and reminisce about the past.

美姑彝族婚礼上有许多有趣的事：背新娘、泼水、喝泡水酒、吃大块肉条、唱对歌、说确（意为男女嬉戏）、聘礼金、约拉古（回娘家）等仪式。其婚礼独具一格，趣味十足。

A Yi wedding in Meigu includes many games and customs: carrying the bride, splashing the bridegroom, drinking Paoshui wine, eating pork strips, singing duets, "Shuo Que" (male-female teasing), offering the bride token, "Yue La Gu" (the bride returning to her parents' home) and so on, making the wedding unique and amusing.

8. 毕摩绘画
Bimo Drawings

第四批国家级非物质文化遗产名录
申报县区及单位：四川省美姑县
Included in the Fourth National Intangible Cultural Heritage List
Declaration county and unit: Meigu County, Sichuan Province

彝族毕摩绘画是由彝族祭司毕摩画在纸张或兽皮、树皮、竹简、石头、木板等载体上的图画，是一种通过绘画与文字相互配合的形式来叙述故事、塑造形象、抒发情感、反映历史生活、表达志向和愿望的艺术体系，是彝族远古绘画艺术的"活化石"，具有鲜明的民族特色。

Bimo drawings are drawings depicting Yi priests, or "Bimo", on such media as paper, animal skin, bamboo and stone or wood plates. As an art by which people tell stories, create images, express feelings, reflect on history and life, and express hope through the combination of images and characters, it is a "living fossil" of ancient Yi art and an intangible heritage with distinct national characteristics.

毕摩是彝族远古"神权"时期的部落酋长，后来逐步蜕变为专掌祭祀、载史、占卜之职的祭司，同时也是彝族民间唯一掌握着系统的原始绘画艺术与文字的人物。毕摩绘画分布于川、滇、黔、桂等地的彝族民间，以大小凉山为分布重点。

The Bimo were tribal chiefs of the Yi ethnic group in the "theocratic" period and later gradually became priests specializing in sacrificial rites, historical records and divination. They were also the first members of the Yi nationality to master the systematic primitive art of painting and writing. Bimo drawings are found among the Yi settlements of Sichuan, Yunnan, Guizhou and Guangxi, with concentrations in the Liangshan Mountains.

毕摩通常以竹、木削制成笔，蘸沾牲血调锅烟灰制成的墨汁，在纸上或木板上进行绘画，且不打草稿，凝神定气，一气呵成，不加雕琢，线条简约。毕摩绘画通常分为两类：一是毕摩文献上的插画图解，二是在木板、石板上的图画符号。毕摩绘画具有以下特征：一是功利性和信仰性；二是原始性；三是独特性；四是书画合一性。2014年，毕摩绘画经国务院批准列入第四批国家级非物质文化遗产名录。

A Bimo usually uses bamboo and wood to make a pen, dips it in ink made from a mixture of ashes and animal blood, and draws on paper or wood without drafting. After a smooth and concentrated process, a drawing is finished in simple primitive lines. There are two types of drawings made by Bimos: the illustrations in Bimo's literature and signs on wood and stone plates. Bimo drawings are characterized by their association with utility and religion; unique and primitive in style, they combine painting and calligraphy. In 2014, Bimo drawings were approved by the State Council for inclusion in the fourth National Intangible Cultural Heritage List.

9. 彝族服饰
Yi Costumes

第四批国家级非物质文化遗产名录

申报县区及单位：四川省昭觉县

Included in the Fourth National Intangible Cultural Heritage List

Declaration county and unit: Zhaojue County, Sichuan Province

凉山型服饰主要流行于四川省凉山彝族自治州和毗邻各地，以及云南省金沙江流域南岸。以被誉为彝族服饰文化艺术之乡的四川省凉山州昭觉县为中心，向四周辐射到彝族北部方言区的圣扎、义诺等各方言土语区，汇集了凉山彝族地区的服饰及服饰文化艺术。凉山彝族服饰随着不同地域、生态和方言而各具特色。

Liangshan-style Yi costumes are mainly popular in the Liangshan Yi Autonomous Prefecture of Sichuan and it's neighboring areas, as well as the southern bank of Jinsha River Valley in Yunnan, and centered around Zhaojue County which is known as the "hometown of Yi costumes". Their influence reaches Shengza, Yinuo and other local dialect areas in the northern Yi dialect area, highlighting the costume style in the Yi settlements of Liangshan. The features of the costumes vary according to region, ecology and dialect.

彝族服饰工艺的主要特点是"做花"工艺。彝族服饰在衣服的衣领、衣襟、袖臂、项背、下摆、裤筒、裤脚、帽子、头帕、挂包、围腰、裙边等部位装饰各种花纹，最常用的工艺习俗有贴花、挑花、穿花、锁花、盘花、补花以及刺绣、滚绣等。

The most distinctive features of Yi costumes lie in the decoration techniques. They are decorated with various patterns on the collar, skirt, armband, back, hem, trouser leg, hat, headband, bag, waistband, skirt hem, etc. The most commonly used decoration techniques are sticking, picking-out, sewing, fixing, supplementing and embroidering.

由彝族服饰可以看出年龄、性别、婚育等差异，还能看出节庆、婚礼、丧葬、崇尚、信仰、礼仪等习俗。彝族女孩长到一定年龄时要举行换裙仪式，表示女孩已成人。彝族老年人丧服面料忌使用色彩鲜艳的红黄两色，多用黑白两色。并在灵堂下方及两侧挂礼服以示祭奠；婚礼新娘装，头缠黑、青布帕，饰以金花银泡，上盖一块头巾，颈饰为银领牌，耳坠为银饰品，上身着绣花宽袖长衣，下着百褶裙，首饰为金银手镯及金银戒指，外披蓝色双层披毡等华丽盛装。

A certain costume can show differences in age, gender, marital status and parental status and beliefs, as well as different kinds for festivals, weddings, funerals, worship, rituals and other customs. A Yi girl attends a costume changing ceremony when they reach a certain age, indicating that she has become an adult. For senior Yi people, two bright colors of red and yellow cannot be used in their mourning apparels; instead, black and white are used. At a memorial service, formal clothes are hung over and on both sides of the room to show respect to the deceased person. At a wedding, the gorgeous bridal costume consists of a black and green headband decorated with gold and silver baubles with a turban, a silver collar at the neck, a pair of silver earrings, a long embroidered dress with wide sleeves, a pleated skirt, gold and silver bracelets and rings, and a double shawl.

正如郭沫若先生所说："由服饰，可以考见民族文化发展的轨迹和各兄弟民族间的相互影响，历代生产方式、阶级关系、风俗习惯、文物制度等，大可一目了然，是绝好的史料。"彝族服饰是穿在身上的历史，是民族工艺中的一颗闪亮明珠。

As Mr. Guo Moruo said, "From costumes we can see the history of national culture, mutual influence among different ethinic groups, production methods, class affiliations, customs, cultural relic systems, etc. of all previous dynasties at a glance. They are excellent historical records." Yi costumes are wearable history and a treasure of folk craftsmanship.

10. 朵乐荷

Duolehe

第一批四川省省级非物质文化遗产名录

申报县区及单位：凉山州普格县人民政府、凉山州布拖县人民政府

Included in the First Sichuan Provincial Intangible Cultural Heritage List

Declaration county and unit: Puge County People's Government and Butuo County

People's Government of Liangshan Prefecture

　　四川凉山彝族火把节中，唯一由女性群体表演的歌舞叫作"朵乐荷"，彝语又称"都火"。她浓郁的民族风格和绚丽的地方特色，丰富而深刻的社会内涵，千百年绵延不辍，存留着原始歌舞的遗风古貌。朵乐荷表演形式是由彝族姑娘们手撑金黄色的油伞，身穿节日盛装，在火把场围成一个个大小不一的圆圈，少则十数人，多则数十上百人。表演者手牵彩巾，唱着传统歌谣，一人领唱领舞，众人重复合应，边唱边走，舞队向顺时针方向转动。德高望重的彝族老人就在其间挑选出火把节上的美女。这一表演总称为"朵乐荷"，歌的内容有：

At the Torch Festival, there is a group dance performed by female dancers called "Duolehe", or "Du Huo" in the Yi language. It features strong national and local styles with deep social connotations, and retains an ancient appearance. To perform the Duolehe, beautifully costumed Yi girls hold golden umbrellas and colorful handkerchiefs, stand in a circle around a bonfire and sing folk songs. The number of dancers ranges from ten to more than a hundred. There is a leading singer and dancer to whom the others respond, singing and dancing clockwise. A highly respected Yi senior will pick out the queen of the festival from among the dancers. The performance as a whole is called "Duolehe" and includes different kinds of songs:

（1）祭祀、祝福性的，如：《朵乐荷》《欧俄欧阿》《荣洛灯》《格拉》；

（1）Sacred songs, including *Duolehe*, *Oueoua*, *Rongluodeng* and *Gela*;

（2）歌舞性的，又称"都荷调"；

（2）Musical songs, also known as *Duhediao*;

（3）传承远古生活及习俗，歌唱生活，感受远古与现实变化的《约约经》；

（3）Songs that inherit customs, sing for life and express historical changes, such as *Yueyuejing*;

（4）结合心境，歌唱及控诉彝族妇女凄惨命运的《阿莫尼惹》；

（4）Songs that express pity for Yi women, such as *Amonire*;

（5）用即兴、比拟和赋兴手法戏谑的《阿依嬷霞》等10余种曲调，若干首歌曲。

（5）Playful songs that feature improvisation, metaphors and wild imagination, including more than 10 melodies and songs, such as *Ayimoxia*.

朵乐荷的歌舞形式、歌唱方式、舞步姿态、队形队列、道具用物等，都有一定习俗和惯例。所唱的歌曲和内容也都有传统的范围。

There are rules for the musical forms, singing, moves, positions, props, etc. of Duolehe. The songs and cotents are also traditionally defined.

朵乐荷保持了原始艺术"三一致"（诗、歌、舞一体）的古朴风貌和形式，是活的历史遗存，具有丰富的文化内涵和社会科学价值，同时是民族内聚力的精神产物，对于构建和谐社会、促进民族团结具有极其重要的意义。

Duolehe inherits a primitive art form combining poetry and music. It is a living historical relic of great social and scientific value, and a symbol of national cohesion. It is of great significance for building a harmonious society and promoting national unity.

11. 民族乐器制作技艺（彝族月琴制作技艺）
National Instrument (Yueqin) Manufacturing Process

第二批四川省省级非物质文化遗产扩展项目名录
申报县区及单位：凉山彝族自治州雷波县文化馆
Included in the Second Sichuan Provincial Intangible Cultural Heritage Extension
Project List
Declaration county and unit: Leibo County Cultural Center, Liangshan Yi
Autonomous Prefecture

凉山彝族"男弹月琴，女弹口弦"是一项广泛流传的习俗。月琴是凉山彝族有代表性的乐器，深受彝族人民喜爱。在长期流传中，月琴音乐的艺术水平和音乐文化两个方面的发展都达到了相当的高度。

In Liangshan, it is customary that men play the yueqin and women play the mouth harp. The yueqin is a representative Yi instrument in Liangshan which is deeply loved by the Yi nationality. Over time, yueqin music has achieved high artistic and cultural levels.

月琴是一种结构科学完整、性能良好、音色优美、表现力强的旋律乐器。彝族月琴音乐不仅资源丰富而且艺术性很高。凉山彝族的民族情感、思想情绪、伦理道德、审美观念，反映在月琴音乐方面的文化现象，主要表现为有关的传说、故事、谚语、乐语、歌谣等，也反映出月琴及音乐在人们心目中和社会生活中的影响。如彝文古籍《西南彝志》描述古代歌场有"蜘蛛弹弦子，苍蝇吹号筒"之句。彝族乐谚"黑溪略撒弦子哦"，意思是"心里的愁与乐，月琴弹出来""口弦会说话，月琴会唱歌。"普格县流传着姑娘史娾与

小伙子拉惹的爱情悲剧，史娓被逼殉情自缢于他二人经常幽会的大树下，拉惹砍下那棵树做成了月琴，因此，彝族人民把月琴视为忠贞爱情的产物。此外，月琴广泛用于社会生活的多种场合，称得上是彝族离不开的精神食粮。

The yueqin is a melodic instrument with a structure of scientific integrity which offers good performance, beautiful timbre and strong expressiveness. As mentioned above, is not only rich in resources but also highly artistic. The emotions, thoughts, ethics and aesthetic concepts of the Yi nationality are reflected in their music such forms as legends, stories, proverbs, songs and so on. This also reflects the role of the yueqin in people's minds and social life. For example, the ancient *Ethnography of the Southwest Yi Nationality* describes a musical scene as "spiders play strings and flies play trumpets." There are old sayings that mean "express your sorrow and joy with a yueqin" "the mouth harp can speak" and "the yueqin can sing". In the love tragedy of the girl Shiwei and the boy Lare which is well-known in Puge County, the girl was forced to die under their rendezvous tree, so the boy cut the tree down and made a yueqin. The Yi nationality consider the yueqin a token of love. The instrument is also widely used on their social occasions. It a must-have item in the lives of Yi nationality.

12. 酿造酒传统酿造技艺（彝族燕麦酒古法酿造技艺）
Traditional Oat Wine Making Techniques

第二批四川省省级非物质文化遗产扩展项目名录
申报县区及单位：凉山彝族自治州会东县文化馆
Included in the Second Sichuan Provincial Intangible Cultural Heritage Extension
Project List
Declaration county and unit: Huidong County Cultural Center, Liangshan Yi
Autonomous Prefecture

　　彝族燕麦酒古法酿造工艺是会东县彝族特有的技艺。对彝族人民来说，酒的价值有时与人的价值相提并论，彝族谚语云："一个人值一匹马，一匹马值一杯酒。"体现了彝族人爽朗、豪放、无酒不成事的习俗。会东县彝族燕麦酒古法酿造工艺，因其浓郁的酒文化而历史十分悠久，古时多数以自酿自足的状态存在，偶尔在彝区以物换物的形式出现。

　　The unique oat wine making techniques of the Yi nationality come from the ancient Yi methods of Huidong County. In Yi culture, wine can sometimes be equal to people in value. A Yi saying goes that "a person is worth a horse, and a horse is worth a glass of wine", representing the hearty character of the Yi nationality and the importance of wine in their culture. The oat wine making techniques of Huidong County have survived throughout history by virtue of its rich wine culture. In ancient times, people made wine to satisfy their own needs, and sometimes traded wine for other goods.

　　彝族人称"有酒便是席"，彝家谚语云："所木拉九以，诺木支几以

（汉区以茶为敬，彝区以酒为尊）。"在彝家，每当客人来到，无沏茶敬客之礼，却有斟酒敬宾之俗。每逢婚嫁，以"酒足"为敬，"饭饱"则次之。彝族酿酒工艺大致分为三种：一是甜酒，彝族称"支边"，类似汉族的醪糟。二是蒸馏酒，彝族称"支儿"，汉族称为白酒。三是泡水酒，即彝族什扎地区盛行的杆杆酒。而会东彝族的燕麦酒属蒸馏酒，被称为转转酒，是会东特有的彝族酿酒工艺和独特的阿都地区饮俗文化。

The Yi nationality believe that "wine alone is sufficient to make a feast",and a Yi proverb holds that Han nationality value tea while Yi nationality value wine. When a Yi household entertains guests, they never pour tea but wine. At a wedding, the importance of "drinking enough" precedes that of "having enough food". There are generally three types of wine: the first is sweet wine, known as "Zhibian" in the Yi language, which is similar to the fermented glutinous rice wine favored by the Han nationality; the second is tequila, known as "Zhiji" to the Yi and as "distilled spirit" to the Han; and the third is "Paoshui", the "ganganjiu" wine popular in Shizha. The oat wine of Huidong County is known for the custom in which everyone sits in circle and drinks in any place. The wine making process and culture of Huidong are unique.

会东县彝族燕麦酒古法酿造出的燕麦酒清香甘醇，不添加第三方原料，不上头，是纯天然原料和原始工艺加工的绿色饮品，所以具有广阔的市场价值和经济价值。酒是彝族人与祖先对话的桥梁，彝族人过年过节通过供奉美酒祭祖献灵，祈求祖先保佑后人远离灾难、六畜兴旺、家门发达；酒是彝族人走亲访友的最佳礼品，也是排解家族矛盾纠纷的溶化剂，更是毕摩、苏尼占卜测卦的法宝。彝人古俗不滥酒，谚语云："酒好只需一杯，贤子只要一个。""男人命不好娶个胃疼妻，女人命不好嫁个酗酒夫。"这就是彝族人的"节饮"思想。

The wine made according to ancient techniques is aromatic, sweet, additive-free and aftereffect-free. Made from natural materials with time-honored methods, the wine is organic produce with bright market prospects and great economic value. Yi nationality use wine to pay tribute to their ancestors. They worship their gods and ancestors by offering wine at festivals and praying for good fortune. Wine is a perfect gift when visiting relatives and friends, a magic potion for resolving disagreements among family members and a tool for the Bimo and Suni to use in practicing divination. Many Yi proverbs refer to wine, such as "a glass of good wine satisfies, and so does a good son", and "A man whose wife has a stomachache is unlucky, and a woman whose husband drinks is unlucky"; this shows the attitude of the Yi nationality towards temperance.

攀枝花市

PANZHIHUA CITY

铜火锅烹饪技艺

苴却石雕刻技艺

大田镇板凳龙

1. 新山傈僳族约德节

Xinshan Lisu Nationality Yuede Festival

第一批四川省省级非物质文化遗产名录

申报县区及单位：米易县文化馆

Included in the First Sichuan Provincial Intangible Cultural Heritage List

Declaration county and unit: Miyi County Cultural Center

　　米易县新山乡是一个傈僳族乡镇，这里居住的傈僳族人大多数是于明、清时期从云南丽江地区迁入的。新山乡的傈僳族是一个一步跨千年的民族，至1950年解放时，他们还处于原始公社状态，没有阶级，没有剥削，没有私有财产的观念，以打猎和采集为生。解放后，在党和政府的大力扶持下，这里的傈僳族人才开始种植粮食，养殖牲畜家禽，渐渐融入现代社会。

Xinshan Township in Miyi County is a Lisu nationality township. Most of the Lisu living here moved from Lijiang in Yunnan Province during the Ming and Qing Dynasties. The Lisu of Xinshan Township form a nationality that has lasted for over 1,000 years. By the time they were liberated in 1950, they were still living in a primitive commune without class, exploitation or the notion of private property. They lived by hunting and gathering. After their liberation, with the strong support of the Party and government, the Lisu people in this area began to grow grain and raise livestock and poultry, and they have since gradually integrated into modern society.

　　每年的农历三月十二至十八日是新山傈僳族人的"约德节"。"约德"是约会的意思，"约德节"就是约会节，即我们所说的情人节。阳春三月的新山，万物复苏、百鸟争鸣，漫山遍野的马缨花次第开放，缤纷绚烂的花朵争奇斗艳，景色美不胜收，正是最适合谈情说爱的季节。

The "Yuede Festival" of the Lisu nationality is held in Xinshan on the 12th to 18th day of the third lunar month each year. As "Yuede" means "dating", "Yuede Festival" means "Dating Festival", namely Valentine's Day. In Xinshan during the third lunar month, everything comes back to life, a hundred birds contend in singing and lantanas blossom all over the mountains and plains. Brilliant and gorgeous flowers compete in beauty and splendor. The scenery is extremely beautiful, making it the most suitable season for love and romance.

"约德节"来临，家家户户的青年男女都精心地打扮自己，姑娘们穿上华美的盛装，小伙子带上心爱的葫芦笙齐聚到一起，唱起优美的山歌，吹起多情的葫芦笙，跳起欢快的锅庄，传递着他们对美好生活的热爱，有情人则趁此良机互诉衷肠，表达爱意。

With the coming of the Yuede Festival, young men and women from every household dress themselves up carefully, and the girls dress in gorgeous costumes. The young men gather together with their beloved Hulusheng (gourd instruments), sing beautiful folk songs, play sonorous melodies and dance the cheerful Guozhuang to convey their wish for a better life. Lovers take this opportunity to express their love and affection.

2. 四川洞经音乐（迤沙拉谈经古乐）
Sichuan Dongjing Music (Yishala Tanjing Ancient Music)

第二批四川省省级非物质文化遗产名录
申报县区及单位：攀枝花市仁和区文化馆
Included in the Second Sichuan Provincial Intangible Cultural Heritage List
Declaration county and unit: Renhe District Cultural Center, Panzhihua City

在"中国历史文化名村""中国俚濮彝族第一寨"——攀枝花市仁和区平地镇迤沙拉村，流传着一种独特的洞经音乐，被称作"迤沙拉谈经古乐"。"谈经古乐"，又称"洞音""儒门洞音""赕经调子"，因以《太上无极总真文昌大洞仙经》为其主要唱诵经文而得名，是一个主要在川、滇地区流传的古老乐种，沿于道教的宗教祭祀仪式，后为儒、释、道三教共用，进而流传到民间，为普通老百姓所用，数百年久传不衰。史料记载，在四川西南角与云南相邻的部分地区，最迟自清代中晚期便有洞经音乐流传。

In Yishala Village of Pingdi Town, Renhe District, Panzhihua City, a "Famous Chinese Historical and Cultural Village" and the "First Village of the Lipu people of Yi Nationality in China", there is a unique form of Dongjing music called

"Yishala Tanjing Ancient Music". Also known as "Dongyin" "Rumendongyin" and "Danjingdiaozi", and named after the primary vocal scriptures of the *Taishangwuji Zongzhen Wenchang Dadong Xianjing*, "Tanjing Ancient Music" is a form of ancient music which is mainly found in the Sichuan and Yunnan regions. Following the religious fete ceremony of Taoism, it was shared by Confucianism, Buddhism and Taoism, and then spread to the people. Having become popular among ordinary people, it has since been inherited for hundreds of years. According to the historical records, in certain areas in the southwestern corner of Sichuan adjacent to Yunnan, Dongjing music has been around since the middle and late Qing Dynasty at the latest.

流传在攀枝花市迤沙拉一带的谈经古乐不是纯粹的洞经音乐，它既有洞经音乐的前身，也有宫廷音乐的悠扬婉转，还有江南水乡的小调韵味。这是因为迤沙拉的彝族俚濮人祖先是明朝洪武十四年（1381）前后陆续从南京应天府、湖南长沙三阴县等地作为军人受命军屯来的其中一部分，以南京应天府来的居多。他们带来家乡的文化，与当地彝族文化交融，这也是迤沙拉谈经古乐与其他洞经音乐不同的原因。谈经古乐以其独特的艺术感染力，深受民间喜爱，逐渐被推广运用在民间的各种庆典活动中，如庙会、寿宴、丧葬仪式等，成为俚濮人生活中不可缺少的组成部分。其演奏形式以齐奏为主，内容可分为生产、生活、战争、风俗的民间欢乐古乐曲；是表达俚濮人宗教信仰、祭祀神灵、祈求上苍赐予幸福的民间谈经古乐曲。

The Tanjing Ancient Music of Yishala in Panzhihua City is not pure Dongjing music. Its predecessor is not only Dongjing music but also the melodious and graceful palace music, as well as the lingering minor key charm of the Yangtze River Delta. This is because the ancestors of the Lipu people in Yishala successively came from Yingtian Prefecture in Nanjing, Sanyin County of Changsha, Hunan Province and other regions as part of the army's command to settle down around the 14th year of the reign of Emperor Hongwu in the Ming Dynasty (1381). The majority came from Yingtian Prefecture in Nanjing. They brought the culture of

their hometowns and it blended with the local indigenous Yi culture, which explains the differences between Yishala Tanjing Ancient Music and other Dongjing music. Deeply loved by the people for its unique artistic appeal, Tanjing Ancient Music has been gradually popularized and used in various folk celebrations such as temple fairs, birthday banquets, funeral ceremonies, etc., and has become an indispensable part of life for Lipu people. Mainly performed in choruses, its contents can be divided into joyous ancient folk music which speaks of production, life, war and customs; it is a form of ancient folk music which expresses the religious beliefs of the Lipu people, including making sacrifices to the gods and praying to Heaven for happiness.

3. 阿署达彝族打跳舞
Ashuda Yi Datiao Dance

第二批四川省省级非物质文化遗产名录
申报县区及单位：攀枝花市东区文化馆
Included in the Second Sichuan Provincial Intangible Cultural Heritage List
Declaration county and unit: East District Cultural center, Panzhihua City

攀枝花市东区银江镇阿署达村是散落于深山之中的一颗明珠。这里居住的民族的先祖为明朝重臣，于洪武开滇之时来到云南，后因犯错被流放到现在的阿署达地区，早期以打猎为生。其后代散居于金沙江沿岸的阿署达、倮果、密地、沙坝等地。

Ashuda Village of Yinjiang Town in the East District of Panzhihua City is a pearl hidden deep in the mountains. The ancestors of the indigenous minorities here were important ministers of the Ming Dynasty. They came to Yunnan when the Hongwu Emperor opened up the province. They were then exiled to the modern-day Ashuda region as punishment for making mistakes. In the early days, they lived through hunting. Their descendants are scattered over Ashuda, Luoguo, Midi, Shaba and other places along the banks of Jinsha River.

流传于阿署达地区的彝族打跳舞与金沙江两岸各族的"锅庄"既同源而又自成体系，已有三四百年的历史，是研究大小凉山民族舞蹈渊源及发展的珍贵素材，是金沙江文化中的重要组成部分。其曲调多样，音乐形象鲜明，时而刚劲有力，时而舒缓深情，时而热烈奔放，时而活泼俏皮，具有突出的民族音乐个性。舞步变换复杂，分三脚、四脚、五脚以至九脚，同时辅以勾、踢、盘、跳、踏等，动作舒展有力、粗犷大方，表现出彝族人火热奔放的性格。原有曲调上百曲，历经几百年的变迁，现尚存能吹能跳的曲调仅40余种，有"一根竹子砍三刀调""四脚儿刨土调""蚕豆芽调""马调""黄鹰闪翅调"等。

The Yi Datiao Dance of the Ashuda region is homologous and self-contained like the "Guozhuang" of all minorities on both banks of Jinsha River. With a history of three to four hundred years, it is a precious resource for studying the origin and development of national dances in Daliangshan and Xiaoliangshan, and an important part of Jinsha River culture. With various melodies and distinct musical characteristics, it is sometimes vigorous and powerful, sometimes soothing and emotional, sometimes passionate and unrestrained, and sometimes lively and witty, with a prominent national music personality. The dance steps are complicated in their movements, divided into three steps, four steps, five steps and even nine steps, and supplemented by hooks, kicks, crosses, jumps, steps and so on. The movements are not only limber and powerful but also rough and generous, showing the passionate and unrestrained character of the Yi nationality. There are 100 songs in the original melody. After several hundred years of vicissitudes, only about 40 tunes can be played to accompany the dance, such as "Yigenzhuzikansandao Tune" "Sijiaoerpaotu Tune" "Candouya Tune" "Ma Tune" "Huangyingshanchi Tune" and so on.

4. 傈僳族婚礼
Lisu Nationality Wedding

第三批四川省省级非物质文化遗产名录
申报县区及单位：攀枝花市盐边县文化馆
Included in the Third Sichuan Provincial Intangible Cultural Heritage List
Declaration county and unit: Yanbian County Cultural Center, Panzhihua City

傈僳族认为土地在于承载万物，婚姻的根本是延续人类并传承先辈意志。盐边县箐河傈僳族乡的傈僳族人，至今仍然保留着他们传统的婚礼习俗。傈僳族家庭为父系一夫一妻制，婚姻由父母包办。儿子娶亲、女儿出嫁后就与父母分居独立生活，幼子和独子留在父母身边传承家业。女子15岁后便"成年"，可定亲。往往由男家舅舅、姑爷或弟弟、表兄弟担任"瓦喇帕"（媒人），带礼品到女家做媒唱"说媒歌"议亲。

The Lisu nationality believe that the land is the carrier of all things and the root of marriage is the continuation of human beings and the transmission of their ancestors' wills. The Lisu nationality of Lisu Township in Qinghe, Yanbian County have retained their traditional wedding customs to the present. The Lisu family is a monogamy of the paternal line, and marriages are arranged by the parents. Sons and daughters live separately from their parents when they get married. The youngest and only child stay with their parents to inherit and pass on their family fortune. When a girl is 15 years old, she will become an "adult" and can be engaged. The bridegroom's uncle, brother or cousin will serve as the "Walapa" (matchmaker), who often brings gifts to the bride's home and sings the "matchmaker song".

迎娶时由东巴先生选择"吉日"，媒人率接亲队伍到女方家，对歌、跳锅庄狂欢，第二天接亲上路。女方家发亲时，由乐手吹奏葫芦笙带领送亲队伍到男方家。上坡、下坎、过沟、过桥时，媒人与送亲客都要对歌。进入男方家后，天黑举行婚礼和盛大的篝火锅庄舞，屋内烧杠香和豆瓣香避邪。第三天新娘、新郎送走客人就到女方家回门，待回门转来，才能同房。整个婚礼为期三天，第一天称为"相帮"，第二天为"正酒"，第三天称为"复原"。婚后一段时间，男方家要向女方家送四件礼品，女方家需回赠牛羊。生子时，女婿抱一只公鸡到岳父母家报喜，生女抱母鸡报喜。若夫妻感情破裂，便各自一方，相互不来往；如丧偶，男可再娶，女可再嫁。

When marrying, Mr. Dongba chooses an "auspicious day". The matchmaker leads the team to pick up the bride at the bride's house, singing songs and dancing Guozhuang, and picks up the bride on the road the next day. When sending the bride from her home, Hulusheng players lead the team accompanying the bride to the bridegroom's home. When climbing up and down hills and crossing ditches and bridges, the matchmakers sing in an antiphonal style with the people accompanying the bride to the bridegroom's family. After entering into the bridegroom's home, the wedding ceremony and grand bonfire Guozhuang dance are held after dark. Incense sticks and bean paste are burned to ward off evil spirits. On the third day, the bride and bridegroom see off their guests and return to the home of the bride's mother. After returning to the bridal chamber, they can consummate the marriage. The whole wedding lasts three days. The first day is called "Xiangbang", the second "Zhengjiu" and the third "Fuyuan". After the wedding, the bridegroom's family will send four gifts to the woman, and the bride's family must give cows and sheep in return. When a son is born, the son-in-law takes a rooster to the father and mother-in-law's home to announce the good news. When a daughter is born, the son-in-law takes a hen. If a couple's relationship breaks down, they will be separated; if they are widowed, the man can remarry, the woman can remarry.

　　傈僳族婚礼整个过程极富传统，它将民族节日、民族歌舞、民族音乐、民族礼仪、民族服饰展示融为一体，是傈僳族生活的重要组成部分，是傈僳族民族文化的典型表现。

　　The whole process of a Lisu wedding is very traditional. It integrates national festivals, folk songs and dances, folk music, national etiquette and national costume display. It is an important part of the Lisu nationality's lives and a typical manifestation of Lisu culture.

5. 仡佬族送年节

Gelao Nationality Songnian Festival

第三批四川省省级非物质文化遗产名录

申报县区及单位：攀枝花市盐边县文化馆

Included in the Third Sichuan Provincial Intangible Cultural Heritage list

Declaration county and unit: Yanbian County Cultural Center, Panzhihua City

　　盐边县的"永兴"古称"喇撒田"，于明朝嘉靖年间建立集镇，是茶马古道上一个重要的驿站。居住在该镇新民村（古称"巴鄂"，也称"八爱"）的仡佬族，他们自称"耶倮"。

　　With the ancient name "Lasatian", "Yongxing" of Yanbian County is a market town established during the reign of Emperor Jiajing in the Ming Dynasty which was an important station for Ancient Tea and Horse Road. The Gelao nationality of Xinmin Village in Yongxing (known as "Ba'e" in ancient times, and also known as "Ba'ai") call themselves "Yeluo".

据本族老人口述：耶俣祖上居住在雅州（今雅安），明朝洪武年间有八兄弟因战乱颠沛流离来到喇撒田河谷，八人同时爱上了这个地方并留下定居，故取地名为"八爱"，距今有700年历史。仡佬族认为：村子住着人，也住着神，人离不开神，神也离不开人，神树、神山、神灵是他们生命中的一部分。

According to oral accounts by old people, the ancestors of Yeluo lived in Yazhou (today's Ya'an). During the reign of Emperor Hongwu in the Ming Dynasty, war forced eight brothers to wander to the valley of Lasatian. All eight of them fell in love with the place, settled down there and named it "Ba'ai", and it now has a history of 700 years. Gelao nationality believe that both people and gods inhabit the village, and that people cannot be separated from gods. The sacred trees, holy mountains and gods form part of their lives.

"送年节"是耶俣沿袭至今的祭祀神灵祖宗、崇拜自然、庆祝丰收、辞旧迎新、保佑平安、凝集族人的传统盛典，是仡佬族人最重要的节日。每年正月初六，庇牟（汉语称东巴或和尚）指派年轻的后生上山采集七种不同的野花枝，打上掌盘，背上背篓到村子里挨家挨户收集族人自愿捐出的钱物，购买鞭炮和祭祀用品。初七一大早，庇牟领着全族人带上预先酿造的"砸杆酒"以及肉和祭品一同来到村后林中一株青杠、黄桷、夜蒿为一体的千年古树下，在树上挂上羊头和红绸带，支大锅煮"百家肉"，用七色花枝搭祭祀神坛，用"砸杆酒"、猪肉及祭品祭祀，乞求神灵保佑族人安康，来年风调雨顺，六畜兴旺，五谷丰登。凡年龄满12岁以上女性不能进入祭祀场地。

The "Songnian Festival" is a traditional grand ceremony of the Gelao nationality for offering sacrifices to the gods and ancestors, worshipping nature, celebrating the harvest, ringing out the Old Year, ringing in the New Year, giving blessings for peace and gathering together. It is the most important festival for the Gelao nationality. On the sixth day of the first lunar month of each year, the "Bimou" ("Dongba" or "monk" in Chinese mandarin) assigns young children to go up the mountain and collect seven different kinds of wildflower branches, put them on palm plates, carry baskets on their backs and go door to door in the village collecting money donated by the people, and buy firecrackers and sacrificial offerings. In the early morning of the seventh day, the Bimou leads the whole family to take pre-brewed "Zagan wine", meat and sacrificial offerings to a millennium-old tree in the woods behind the village where green bars, yellow shrubs and night artemisia mingle. A sheep's head and red silk ribbons are hung on the tree, a large pot is used to cook "meat for various families", seven-colored flower branches are used to build a sacrificial altar and the "Zagan wine", meat and sacrificial offerings are used to pray to the gods to protect the people's well-being, next year's favorable weather, thriving domestic animals and a bumper grain harvest. Girls over the age of 12 cannot enter the sacrificial arena.

庇牟烧香拜祖后，开始唱祭祀歌，其大意为：我们住在高山，离天最近，离祖先灵魂最近，远离战乱，相亲相爱；我们住在密林，找吃食最近，离亲人最近，远离纠纷，互帮互助……祭祀过后，在铺有松毛的地上摆上"百家肉"，斟上"砸杆酒"，族人开怀畅饮。老者聚在一起商谈族中大事和传承事宜，妇女们拿出自家刺绣、鞋垫、香包相互赠送祝福，青年们则用火枪、弓箭打靶取乐。夜晚，族人们围着篝火尽情地跳锅庄舞，通宵达旦地狂欢、庆祝节日。

After the Bimou burns incense and worships his ancestors, he begins to sing sacrificial songs with a general theme: we live in the high mountains, nearest to heaven, nearest to the souls of our ancestors and farthest from war, and we love each other; we live in dense forests, nearest to food, nearest to our relatives and farthest from disputes, and we help each other... After the sacrificial ceremony, the "meat for various families" is placed on the ground covered with pine leaves, the "Zagan wine" is poured and the people of the clan drink happily. The old people gather to discuss the great events and inheritance of the tribe. The women take out their own embroidery, insoles and sachets to give each other blessings. The young people use muskets and bows to shoot at targets for fun. At night, people gather around the bonfire happily and dance the Guozhuang to celebrate the festival all night.

6. 大田镇板凳龙

Datian Bench Dragon

第一批攀枝花市市级非物质文化遗产名录
申报县区及单位：攀枝花市仁和区文化馆
Included in the First Panzhihua City Intangible Cultural Heritage List
Declaration county and unit: Renhe District Cultural Center, Panzhihua City

传说在清朝同治年间，仁和区大田镇的银鹿村住着一户赫姓夫妇，夫妇俩老来无子，便到庙里求佛。由于山高路远，老夫妇走得十分困倦，到寺庙时，不由得说了一句："终于走到了，把我的脚都走大了！"果然佛随人意，后夫妇喜得一子，却天生一双大脚，夫妇为其取名赫友禄。由于脚大，人们都叫他赫大脚。赫大脚生性聪颖，特别喜欢唱歌。十来岁时，杨家地主便派他到元谋学艺，几年的时间，吹、拉、弹、唱门门精通，回村后成了银鹿村第一位民间艺人。他召集本地村民就地取材，制作板龙进行舞龙表演，并一直流传下来。

Legend has it that during the reign of Emperor Tongzhi in the Qing Dynasty, a couple surnamed He lived in Yinlu Village of Datian Town, Renhe District. They had no children when they grew old so they went to the temple to pray to the Buddha. The old couple were very tired after a long trek. When they arrived at the temple, they could not help but say, "We have arrived at last with swollen feet!" Sure enough, the Buddha granted their wishes. The couple was blessed with a son, but he was born with a pair of big feet. The son was named He Youlu. Because of his big feet, people called him He Dajiao. He was born smart and especially liked singing songs. When he was in his teens, a landlord surnamed Yang sent him to Yuanmou to study art. In a few years, he was proficient in playing musical instruments and singing. After returning home, he became the first folk artist in Yinlu Village. He summoned the local villagers to use local materials, make bench dragons and perform the dragon dance. This performance has been handed down through the generations.

板凳龙即把龙扎在板凳上，龙用竹子或稻草编成，蒙上彩色的布料。三人合舞一条板凳龙，前面两位是女子，后面一位则为男子。表演时，女士的阴柔之美和男士的阳刚之气合二为一，尽显板凳龙的独特魅力。农闲了，村民们喜欢组织起来跳板凳龙舞，在田间小道、农家院坝都能看到村民把这似龙的板凳举在手中，时而旋转、时而翻滚，在鼓点声中挥洒热情，挥舞出丰收的喜悦和对美好明天的希望。

"Bench Dragon" means tying a dragon to a bench. The dragon is made of bamboo or straw and covered with colored cloth. Three people dance together with a bench dragon, the front two women and the latter one a man. During the performance, the feminine beauty of the women and the masculine spirit of the man combine to show the unique charm of the bench dragon. In the slack season, the villagers like to organize the bench dragon dance. In the fields and farmyards and on dams, villagers can be seen lifting dragon-like benches in their hands, sometimes spinning, sometimes rolling, expressing enthusiasm, the joy of harvest and the hope for a better tomorrow amid the sound of drums.

舞板凳龙阵容可大可小，两三条板凳就可以成舞，几十甚至几百条板凳龙聚在一起则能表现出恢宏磅礴的气势。近年来，攀枝花市文化工作者将挖掘出的板凳龙编排后在"四川省首届冬旅会开幕式""四川省少数民族运动会开幕式""四川省农民健身展示大会"等大型活动上展示，赢得了多方好评。

The cast of the bench dragon dance can be large or small, two or three benches can be used in the dance, and dozens or even hundreds of bench dragons used at the

same time can present magnificent momentum. In recent years, the cultural workers of Panzhihua have arranged for bench dragons to be displayed at the "First Sichuan Winter Tourism Conference Opening Ceremony" "Sichuan Ethnic Minority Sports Games Opening Ceremony" "Sichuan Farmers Fitness Exhibition Conference" and other large-scale activities, which winning high praise for bench dragon.

7. 铜火锅烹饪技艺
Copper Hotpot Cooking Techniques

第二批米易县县级非物质文化遗产名录
申报县区及单位：攀枝花市米易县文化馆
Included in the Second Miyi County Intangible Cultural Heritage List
Declaration county and unit: Miyi County Cultural Center， Panzhihua City

铜火锅，用铜制作的特制锅烹饪，以木炭为燃料，原料主要是土鸡、火腿、生态肉丸、新鲜蔬菜等，风味独特，深受八方食客欢迎。其代表是米易铜火锅。火锅源自上古，在公元前150年左右的《韩诗外传》中记载着的"击钟列鼎"而食，就是火锅的萌芽。北齐《魏书·獠传》记载："铸铜为器，大口宽腹，名曰铜。既薄且轻，易于熟食。"其中的铜器被人认为是铜火锅。

This dish is cooked in a special pot made of copper. Charcoal is used as the fuel and the ingredients mainly comprise local chicken, ham, organic meatballs, fresh vegetables, and so on. It has a unique flavor and is welcomed by diners from all over the world. The representative kind is the Miyi Copper Hotpot. This dish originated in ancient times. The "striking bells and rowing tripods" dish recorded in the *Unauthorized History of Han Poetry* around 150 BC was the prototype of the modern hot pot. In the Northern Qi Dynasty, it was recorded in the Book of the *Wei Dynasty: Biography of Liao* that, "Copper is cast into a device with a large mouth and wide abdomen which is known as a 'copper'. It is thin and light and easy to cook food in." This copper ware has since been identified as a copper hotpot.

米易铜火锅包括底盘、锅身、火座、铜盖、火筒、小盖六个部分，有人推断，米易铜火锅可能是从山西传过来的。关于米易族源，民间一直口口相传着一首妇幼皆知的民谣："问我祖先在何处，山西洪洞大槐树。祖先故居叫什么？大槐树下老鸹窝。"在四川省凉山彝族自治州会理县则有这样的记载，明太祖朱元璋为平定元末叛军，在会理实行军屯，中原一带的士卒带来的中原先进技术、文化，与会理地区特有的，具有良好的抗衰老、抗冻、增强脾胃等功效的红铜巧妙结合，加上特产食材的天然结合，便衍生了独具特色的会理铜火锅。而米易安宁河沿岸大部分地区在很长一段时期都是会理的辖区。时至今日，人们认为米易铜火锅实际上就是会理铜火锅的扩展。作为餐具的铜火锅，过去是一些人家送给女儿的陪嫁，也是父母给分家另过子女的一份财产。现在，生产铜火锅的技艺在米易县已基本消失，所需无一例外地从会理购进。2009年，这种传统制作艺术被列为四川省非物质文化遗产名录，铜火锅烹饪技艺被列入米易县县级非物质文化遗产名录项目，有了代表性传承人。

Miyi Copper Hotpot consists of six parts, namely the base plate, pot body, fire seat, copper lid, torch and small lid. Some people believe that the Miyi Copper Hotpot may have spread from Shanxi. There is a folk song about the origin of the Miyi people which is well known to everyone: "Ask me where my ancestors were, Big Locust Tree in Hongdong, Shanxi Province. What is the name of my ancestral home? The old nest under Big Locust Tree." In Huili County of the Liangshan Yi Autonomous Prefecture, Sichuan Province, such records exist. In order to pacify the remaining rebels at the end of the Yuan Dynasty, Zhu Yuanzhang, the first emperor of the Ming Dynasty, carried out military operations in Huili. The advanced technology and culture brought by the soldiers from the Central Plains were ingeniously combined with red copper, which is unique to the region and has positive properties as anti-aging, anti-freezing and strengthening the spleen and stomach, and the natural combination of specialty food ingredients, thereby giving rise to the unique Huili Copper

Hotpot. Most of the areas along Anning River in Miyi were jurisdictions of Huili for a long time. Today, many people believe that Miyi Copper Hotpot is actually an extension of Huili Copper Hotpot. Copper hotpot tableware used to be the dowry of certain families for their daughters and the property of parents for their separated children. Today the copper hotpot production technology of Miyi County has basically disappeared, and all copper hotpots must be brought from Huili. In 2009, this traditional production art was included in the Intangible Cultural Heritage List of Sichuan Province, and copper hotpot cooking technology was included in the Miyi County Intangible Cultural Heritage List as a representative successor.

　　米易铜火锅，源自民间，居民经常用铜火锅煮食物，补充体内铜元素，在一定程度上能够预防心血管疾病、骨质疏松症和痛风、少白头等疾病。如今，铜火锅已经成为小城引以为豪的一张名片。

Miyi Copper Hotpot originated among the people. They often used a copper pot to cook food in order to supplement the body with copper. It can prevent cardiovascular disease, osteoporosis, gout, premature graying and other diseases to a certain extent. Nowadays, the copper hotpot has become a business card of which the small town is proud.

8. 苴却石雕刻技艺
Juque Ink Stone Carving Techniques

第三批攀枝花市市级非物质文化遗产名录
申报县区及单位：攀枝花市敬如石艺有限责任公司
Included in the Third Panzhihua City Intangible Cultural Heritage List
Declaration county and unit: Panzhihua Jingrushiyi Company, ltd.

苴却砚原石材名为苴却石，产于攀枝花市仁和区平地镇与大龙潭乡之间。苴却石多藏身于万丈悬崖之上，地形险峻，开采艰难，它的石材、石质、石品集中国四大名砚优点于一体，堪称中华一绝、攀西奇葩。

The raw stone material of Juque ink stone is named "Juque stone" and produced between Pingdi Town and Dalongtan Township in Renhe District, Panzhihua City. Most Juque stone is hidden among dizzying cliffs in the dangerously steep terrain, making it difficult to gather. It's material, texture and quality contain all the merits of the four famous ink stones of China, and can be called a unique article in the country and a rare article of Western Panzhihua.

苴却砚雕刻工艺历史悠久，有着几百年的历史。苴却砚雕刻精美，图案栩栩如生，体现了中国传统石雕技艺的精美绝伦，是最具中国特色的艺术品。清咸丰年间，现攀枝花市大龙潭乡和平地镇一带苴却石产地附近工匠制砚已成系统。1909年，大姚县苴却巡检宋光枢，取砚三方赴巴拿马万国博览会一举获选，苴却砚名震中外。而后因战乱及地理位置偏僻、交通运输等诸多因素匿迹多年，直到20世纪80年代，随着攀枝花地区的开发建设，沉寂多年的苴却石材，在各方的努力下，再次被挖掘出来，得以开发保护并重放异彩。

The Juque ink stone carving techniques have a long history of several hundred years. The fine carvings and vivid patterns of Juque ink stones embody exquisite traditional Chinese stone carving techniques, and stand among the most distinctive art works with Chinese characteristics. During the reign of Emperor Xianfeng in the Qing Dynasty, the artisan ink stone system near the origin of Juque stone in today's Dalongtan Township and Pingdi Town, Panzhihua City, was established. In 1909, Dayao County Juque Inspector Song Guangshu took three ink stones to the Panama–Pacific International Exposition; all three were elected in one stroke and Juque ink stone became famous at home and abroad. Then, due to war, it's remote geographical location, difficult transportation conditions and many other factors, Juque stone disappeared for many years. In the 1980s, with the development and construction of the Panzhihua region, the Juque stone material which had been silent for so many years was excavated again thanks to the efforts of all parties; it's developed and protected, reproducing its former splendor.

苴却砚是"发墨好、下墨快、宜书画、不损毫"的极品石砚，受到市场极大青睐。近年来，随着石砚的观赏、收藏价值日益提高，攀枝花的艺术家们又创造了苴却石壁挂、摆件、茶盘、文镇、印章、烟缸、笔筒等艺术新品和旅游纪念品，深受人们喜爱。而今苴却砚早已跻身于中国名砚行列，成为每次中外名砚大展中不可缺少的砚种。如今，苴却砚已经成为攀枝花的文化高标，是攀枝花最具特色的文化代表。

Juque ink stone is the best ink stone for "producing fine and glossy ink suitable for calligraphy and painting without damaging the brush", earning it great favor in the market. In recent years, with the increasing ornamental and collectible value of ink stones, Panzhihua artists have created new artistic products including Juque stone wall hangings, decorations, tea trays, paperweights, seals, ashtrays, pen holders and so on. Such tourist souvenirs are deeply loved by the people. Juque ink stone has long been among the ranks of Chinese famous ink stones, becoming an indispensable kind of ink stone in every exhibition of famous Chinese and foreign ink stones. Nowadays, Juque ink stone has become the cultural high standard of Panzhihua and its most distinctive cultural representative.

9. 甘蔗皮酿酒技艺
Sugarcane Skin Wine Making Techniques

第二批米易县县级非物质文化遗产名录

申报县区及单位：米易县文化馆

Included in the Second Miyi County Intangible Cultural Heritage List

Declaration county and unit: Miyi County Cultural Center.

甘蔗皮酿酒又叫渣皮酒。甘蔗有两种，皮色深紫近黑的甘蔗，俗称黑甘蔗，性质较温和滋补，喉痛热盛者不宜；皮色青的青甘蔗，味甘而性凉，有清热之效，能解肺热和肠胃热。

Sugarcane wine is also called "slag skin wine". There are two kinds of sugarcane. Sugarcane with dark purple to dark brown skin, commonly known as black sugarcane, has a mild and nourishing nature, and is not suitable for patients with throat pain or heat excess. Dark green sugarcane is sweet and cool, and has the effect of clearing away heat. It can relieve lung heat and stomach heat.

甘蔗皮酿酒技艺的方法如下：

The methods of sugarcane wine making are as follows:

方法一，纯甘蔗发酵法。选取甘蔗洗干净打碎加入糯米甜曲，1斤甘蔗加入3克糯米甜曲，一般发酵8~12天即可过滤出来。

Method I: the pure sugarcane fermentation method. Select washed and smashed sugarcane, and add sweet yeast from glutinous rice. Add 3 grams of sweet yeast from glutinous rice for every 500 grams of sugarcane. It can be filtered out after generally fermenting for 8 to 12 days.

方法二，生粮混合发酵法。把甘蔗跟粮食混合发酵，选取甘蔗洗干净打碎跟大米混合搅拌均匀，加入高产酒曲，1斤甘蔗粮食混合物加入4克高产酒曲即可。发酵时间也为8~12天，具体的还要看发酵时的温度。甘蔗跟大米的比例可自己调节，甘蔗放得越多，味道越浓，比例一般是30：100，即30斤甘蔗兑100斤大米。发酵完全后，即可用蒸酒设备蒸馏，得出的酒口感纯正，产量高，一般酒厂都采取此方法。

Method II: the fermentation method of mixing raw grains. Mix sugarcane with grain for fermentation; select rice and mix it with washed and smashed sugarcane; stir well and add 4 grams of high-yield distiller's yeast for every 500 grams of grain. The fermentation duration is 8 to 12 days. The fermentation temperature should be also taken into consideration. The ratio of sugarcane to rice can be adjusted at will. The greater the amount of sugarcane, the stronger the flavor. The ratio is generally 30:100, namely 30 jin of sugarcane to 100 jin of rice. After fermentation is complete, it can be distilled with distillation equipment. The wine has a mellow and normal taste, and a high yield. This method is generally adopted by wineries.

方法三，熟料混合发酵法。先把大米煮熟，摊凉至20~30摄氏度，把甘蔗跟大米混合加高产酒曲搅拌均匀，1斤甘蔗粮食混合物加入3克酒曲，装桶发酵，发酵时间同样是8~12天，发酵完全后，即可用蒸酒设备蒸馏出来。

Method III: the fermentation method of mixing cooked materials. Cook the rice and spread and cool it at 20~30°C. Mix the sugarcane and rice together with high-yield yeast and stir well; add 3 grams of yeast for every 500 grams of grain. Barrel it to let it ferment. The fermentation duration is 8 to 12 days. After fermentation is complete, it can be distilled with distillation equipment.

方法四，把按第一种方法做好的酒过滤出来。加入纯大米酒稀释，调酒度。可调节自己喜欢的酒度。甘蔗白酒是采用纯甘蔗汁为原料，通过特殊工艺酿制而成。具有香型特、品质纯正、不易上头（杂醇油含量低）等众多优点。

Method IV: the wine filtration method. Add pure rice wine for dilution; adjust the alcohol content to your preferred level. Sugarcane liquor is made from pure sugarcane juice with special techniques. It has such advantages as a special fragrance, pure quality and no aftereffects (due to its low fusel oil content).

南方丝绸之路四川篇非物质文化遗产项目一览表

非物质文化遗产名录					
序号	项目名称	分布区域	申报单位	项目公布批次	代表性传承人
1	新山傈僳族约德节	攀枝花市米易县新山傈僳族乡	米易县文化馆	第一批四川省省级非物质文化遗产名录	贺国银贺春燕
2	阿署达彝族打跳舞	攀枝花市	东区文化馆	第二批四川省省级非物质文化遗产名录	鲍有志
3	铜火锅烹饪技艺	攀枝花市米易县攀莲镇	米易县文化馆	第二批米易县县级非物质文化遗产名录	张国宾
4	仡佬族送年节	攀枝花市盐边县永兴镇	盐边县文化馆	第三批四川省省级非物质文化遗产名录	熊献青
5	傈僳族婚礼	攀枝花市盐边县菁河傈僳族乡	盐边县文化馆	第三批四川省省级非物质文化遗产名录	谷万里
6	四川洞经音乐（迤沙拉谈经古乐）	攀枝花市仁和区平地镇迤沙拉村	仁和区文化馆	第二批四川省省级非物质文化遗产名录	起光禄
7	大田镇板凳龙	攀枝花市仁和区大田镇银鹿村	仁和区文化馆	第一批攀枝花市市级非物质文化遗产名录	廖国良
8	甘蔗皮酿酒技艺	攀枝花市米易县草场乡碗厂村	米易县文化馆	第二批米易县县级非物质文化遗产名录	王明顺
9	苴却石雕刻技艺	攀枝花市仁和区大龙潭彝族乡、平地镇、总发乡	攀枝花市敬如石艺有限责任公司	第三批攀枝花市市级非物质文化遗产名录	罗伟先罗春明

序号	项目名称	分布区域	申报单位	项目公布批次	代表性传承人
10	蜀绣	四川省成都市	成都非物质文化遗产保护中心	第一批国家级非物质文化遗产名录	孟德芝杨德全郝淑萍
11	蜀锦织造技艺	四川省成都市	蜀锦织绣有限责任公司	第一批国家级非物质文化遗产名录	贺斌刘晨曦叶永洲等
12	成都漆艺	四川省成都市金牛区	成都市漆器工艺厂	第一批国家级非物质文化遗产名录	宋西平尹利萍
13	成都糖画	四川省成都市及周边区域	四川省成都市锦江区文化馆	第二批国家级非物质文化遗产名录	樊德然蔡树全等
14	卓文君与司马相如的故事	成都市邛崃市临邛镇	成都邛崃市	第二批四川省省级非物质文化遗产名录	付尚志
15	鱼凫传说	成都市温江区万春镇报恩村	温江区文化馆	第三批成都市市级非物质文化遗产名录	
16	成都牛儿灯	成都市大邑县新场镇	大邑县文化馆	第三批四川省省级非物质文化遗产名录	王桐林汤朋寿
17	人日游草堂	成都市青羊区杜甫草堂	成都杜甫草堂博物馆	第三批四川省省级非物质文化遗产名录	
18	四川清音	四川省泸州、宜宾为中心，遍及周边区域	四川省成都艺术剧院	第二批国家级非物质文化遗产名录	程永玲田临平
19	四川扬琴	成都、重庆、泸州、自贡等城市和地区	四川省曲艺团、成都艺术剧院、四川省音乐舞蹈研究所	第二批国家级非物质文化遗产名录	曾克蓉付兵林同清等
20	新繁棕编	四川省成都市新都区新繁镇	四川省成都市新都区	第三批国家级非物质文化遗产名录	阙爱军朱木兰高崇洋

非物质文化遗产名录

序号	项目名称	分布区域	申报单位	项目公布批次	代表性传承人
			非物质文化遗产名录		
21	夹关高跷	四川省成都市邛崃市夹关镇	成都市邛崃市群众艺术馆	第三批四川省省级非物质文化遗产名录	郭加权
22	都江堰放水节	四川省都江堰市	都江堰市文体局	第一批国家级非物质文化遗产名录	
23	夫妻肺片传统制作技艺	四川省成都市	四川省成都市饮食公司	第一批四川省省级非物质文化遗产名录	王钦锐
24	竹麻号子	成都市邛崃市平乐镇	成都市邛崃市群众艺术馆	第二批国家级非物质文化遗产名录	杨祚钦
25	西岭山歌	成都市大邑县西岭镇	四川省大邑县	第四批国家级非物质文化遗产名录	张道深任汉成
26	成都道教音乐	成都市青城山道教团体	成都市道教协会	第二批国家级非物质文化遗产名录	董云龙
27	彝族火把节	凉山彝族自治州	凉山彝族自治州	第一批四川省省级非物质文化遗产名录	
28	彝族年	凉山彝族自治州	凉山彝族自治州	第三批国家级非物质文化遗产名录	老板萨龙
29	口弦音乐	四川省布拖县	四川省布拖县	第二批国家级非物质文化遗产名录	马国国
30	甲搓	四川省盐源县	四川省盐源县	第二批国家级非物质文化遗产名录	喇翁基
31	彝族漆器髹饰技艺	四川省喜德县	四川省喜德县	第二批国家级非物质文化遗产名录	吉伍巫且

			非物质文化遗产名录		
序号	项目名称	分布区域	申报单位	项目公布批次	代表性传承人
32	彝族银饰制作技艺	四川省布拖县	四川省布拖县	第二批国家级非物质文化遗产名录	勒古沙日
33	婚俗（彝族传统婚俗）	四川省美姑县	四川省美姑县	第三批国家级非物质文化遗产名录	沈尔阿培
34	毕摩绘画	四川省美姑县	四川省美姑县	第四批国家级非物质文化遗产名录	曲比阿伍
35	彝族服饰	四川省昭觉县	四川省昭觉县	第四批国家级非物质文化遗产名录	曲比克西
36	朵乐荷	凉山州普格县	凉山州普格县	第一批四川省省级非物质文化遗产名录	
37	民族乐器制作技艺（彝族月琴制作技艺）	凉山彝族自治州雷波县	凉山彝族自治州雷波县文化馆	第二批四川省省级非物质文化遗产扩展项目名录	
38	酿造酒传统酿造技艺（彝族燕麦酒古法酿造技艺）	凉山彝族自治州会东县	凉山彝族自治州会东县文化馆	第二批四川省省级非物质文化遗产扩展项目名录	
39	荥经砂器烧制技艺	雅安市荥经县六合乡古城村	四川省荥经县	第二批国家级非物质文化遗产名录	严云杰朱庆平
40	南路边茶制作技艺	四川雅安、天全等地	四川省雅安市	第二批国家级非物质文化遗产名录	李朝贵甘玉祥明玉兰卫国梅树华
41	绿林派武术	青城山、雅安	四川省雅安市雨城区文化馆	第二批四川省省级非物质文化遗产名录	路军健

非物质文化遗产名录				
序号	项目名称	分布区域	申报单位	项目公布批次	代表性传承人
42	汉源彩塑	雅安市汉源县九襄镇	雅安市汉源县文化体育局	第二批四川省省级非物质文化遗产名录	曹润洪
43	荥经民间竹号	雅安市荥经县	雅安市荥经县文化馆	第三批四川省省级非物质文化遗产名录	廖建康
44	抬阁（晏场高台）	雅安市	四川省雅安市雨城区文化馆	第三批四川省省级非物质文化遗产名录	杨昌荣
45	花灯（芦山花灯）	雅安市芦山县	雅安市芦山县文化馆	第二批四川省省级非物质文化遗产扩展项目名录	裴体文
46	家禽菜肴传统烹制技艺（周记棒棒鸡制作技艺）	雅安市荥经县	雅安市荥经县文化馆	第三批四川省省级非物质文化遗产名录	周仕英
47	尔苏木雅藏族《母虎历法》	雅安市石棉县	石棉县文物管理所	第三批雅安市市级非物质文化遗产名录	
48	木雅藏族"什结拉布"	雅安市石棉县	石棉县文物管理所	第三批雅安市市级非物质文化遗产名录	
49	上里镇天灯节	雅安市上里镇	雅安市雨城区	第一批雅安市市级非物质文化遗产名录	
50	马马灯	雅安市名山区	雅安市名山区	第一批雅安市市级非物质文化遗产名录	郑朝仁

参考文献

[1] 宋志辉. 南方丝绸之路经济带与"一带一路"的关系[J]. 一带一路报道,
2017（3）.

[2] 黄俊棚, 龚伟. 论南方丝绸之路与茶马古道的关系——以"邛人故地"为
中心[J]. 中华文化论坛, 2017, 005（5）.

[3] 宋志辉, 蒋真明, 张齐美晨. 南方丝绸之路经济带建设及其与"一带一
路"的关系[J]. 南亚研究季刊, 2016（4）.

[4] 杨昌明. 论蜀绣文化的几个特点[J]. 文史杂志, 2013（2）.

[5] 宋志辉. 南方丝绸之路经济带对西部边疆安全的意义[J]. 西部发展研究,
2015（4）.

[6] 郑莹莹. "印度掠影"成都站系列活动推动两地交流合作进入新阶段[N].
成都日报, 2014-03-16（4）.

[7] 宋志辉, 马春燕. 四川在"南方丝绸之路经济带"建设中的地位和作用[J].
南亚研究季刊, 2014（1）.

[8] 宋志辉, 马春燕. 试析南方丝绸之路在中印关系中的作用[J]. 南亚研究季
刊, 2012（2）.

[9] 杨利君. 浅谈非物质文化遗产项目——蜀绣的传承与保护[J]. 青春岁月,
2011（24）.

[10] 平安, 赵敏. 中国名绣之苏绣和蜀绣[J]. 环球市场信息导报, 2014（32）.

[11] 陈通泉, 黄永建. 成都, 成都文化[J]. 中国集体经济, 2014（17）: 82-93.

[12] 赵敏. 东方明珠——四大名绣之蜀绣[J]. 艺术市场, 2007（7）.

[13] 朱华. 蜀绣文化探讨[J]. 四川丝绸2008（4）.

[14] 张琰, 甘森. 蜀绣活色生香可夺真[J]. 西部广播电视, 2009（4）.